BROADWAY PRESENTS!

Audition | Musical Theatre Anthology

YOUNG MALE EDITION

CDs included

16–32 BAR EXCERPTS FROM STAGE & FILM

Includes Song Set-Up, Audition Tips, Vocal Style & Genre Indexes

Edited & Compiled by **Lisa DeSpain**

Alfred Music Publishing Co., Inc.
16320 Roscoe Blvd., Suite 100
P.O. Box 10003
Van Nuys, CA 91410-0003

Alfred

ISBN 10: 0-7390-7341-9
ISBN 13: 978-0-7390-7341-4

alfred.com

Contents

Introduction

Auditioning is a skill every musical theatre performer must learn. It is through auditioning that a director, casting agent, or teacher becomes familiar your talents and makes the decision of how to cast you in a production. A musical theatre audition begins with the song.

Most auditions ask for a "16" or "32-bar cut," a shortened section of a song. In this small amount of time, it is important to demonstrate both your vocal strengths and your ability to act a song. Every selection in this anthology was crafted to showcase these important skills. Although some selections presented are longer than 16 measures, they are of an appropriate length due to tempo. Longer cuts have an optional starting point part way through.

It is important to match the style of your song to the musical and vocal style of the production. Never sing a song from the production unless specifically asked, but choose a selection that sounds like it is from the same score.

Here are a few suggestions.

1. Determine the year the show or songs in the show were written and choose a song from around the same date. For example, if auditioning for *Pajama Game*, which was written in 1954, "I Met a Girl" from *Bells are Ringing*, composed in 1956 is an excellent choice. Be careful with jukebox musicals, which are shows created using pre-existing songs. For example, although *Mamma Mia!* premiered on Broadway in 2001, the songs were written in the 1970s.

2. Sing a song written by the same composer but from a different show. For example, if auditioning for *My Fair Lady* composed by Alan Jay Lerner and Frederick Loewe, sing a song from *Camelot.*

3. If you have a specific character in mind, choose a song that demonstrates that character's attributes. Og in *Finian's Rainbow* is a comedic role who is confused by love. His big number is "When I'm Not Near the Girl I Love." The song "Love I Hear" from *A Funny Thing Happened on the Way to the Forum* is also comedic and similar in its views on love. Gabey, from *On the Town* is a romantic lead who sings "Lucky to be Me," a dramatic ballad. Sing a dramatic ballad such as "On the Street Where You Live."

4. Many musicals and characters are sung with specific vocal styles: legit, belt, mix or pop/contemporary. You want to match the singing style of the production in your audition song. A vocal teacher is the best resource to clarify these terms and coach you in the appropriate technique.

I've included several indexes to help with choosing your song. I hope this book can be a guide and assist in making the musical decisions for your audition easier.

Break a leg!
Lisa DeSpain

Lisa DeSpain is an Assistant Professor of Music and Theatre at LaGuardia Community College—CUNY (City University of New York) where she serves as Coordinator for the Performing Arts. She is the former Music Director for Professional Performing Arts School, New York City's premiere public school for teens training for performance careers on Broadway.

Song Set Up

21 Guns
American Idiot: The Musical
Johnny, Will, and Tunny have made life choices resulting in terrible consequences. They question their mistakes and wonder about those they have loved and hurt.

All I Care About is Love
Chicago
Billy Flynn, a smooth talking lawyer states his true reason for defending high profile murderesses – love.

All I Need is the Girl
Gypsy
Tulsa is tired of being a chorus boy in Baby June's vaudeville act. He has dreams of being a headliner. All he needs to complete his act is the right girl.

All That's Known
Spring Awakening
Melchior is a young, brilliant teen enrolled in a strict and mind-numbing school. He questions his studies regarding what knowledge is truly important.

Alone in the Universe
Seussical the Musical
Horton and Jojo are feeling misunderstood but soon realize that somebody else out there understands and believes in them.

And They're Off
A New Brain
Gordon remembers his childhood and the conflict between his parents over his father's gambling habit.

Boulevard of Broken Dreams
American Idiot: The Musical
Johnny, a discontented youth from the suburbs wanders through "the city" wondering about a beautiful girl he saw in an apartment window.

Bring Me My Bride
A Funny Thing Happened on the Way to the Forum
Roman Legionnaire Captain Miles Gloriosus is a perfect specimen of manhood. He arrives to claim his bride, the equally perfect female, Philia.

Brush Up Your Shakespeare
Kiss Me Kate
Two gangsters perform a slapstick routine to cheer up the heartbroken director of a musical adaptation of *The Taming of the Shrew*.

C'est Moi
Camelot
Lancelot, an over-confident French knight presents himself at King Arthur's court, assured that his virtues will be an asset to the newly formed Knights of the Round Table.

Come Back to Me
On a Clear Day You Can See Forever
Dr. Marc, a psychiatrist, finally admits he's in love with Daisy, a patient with remarkable E.S.P. Although Daisy has run away from him, Dr. Marc calls her to "come back," knowing she can hear him.

Corner of the Sky
Pippin
Pippin, eldest son of King Charlemagne questions his purpose in life and the meaning of true happiness.

Dames
42nd Street
Billy Lawlor, leading song and dance man performs the opening production number from a fictitious Broadway musical called "Pretty Lady."

Desperado
The singer questions why Desperado chooses to live life as a rebel and if he'd be happier changing his ways.

Different
Honk!
Ugly, an unattractive duckling questions why he looks different from his siblings and wonders why being different is considered a bad thing.

Easy to Love
Anything Goes
Billy, a young banker, expresses his feelings for society debutante Hope, wishing to woo her away from her rich fiancée.

Evenin' Star
110 in the Shade
Starbuck is a con man and drifter. He sings to the evening star, comparing their transient lives.

Everybody Says Don't
Anyone Can Whistle
The mysterious Hapgood questions Nurse Fey's attitude of living according to the prescribed rules. He encourages her to challenge the status quo.

Fit as a Fiddle (and Ready for Love)
Singin' in the Rain
Soon-to-be Hollywood star Don Lockwood and friend Cosmo perform their vaudeville act and are discovered by a moving pictures producer.

Grow For Me
Little Shop of Horrors
Seymour, a lowly flower shop assistant has been nurturing a strange plant named Audrey 2. Finally he discovers what food makes the plant thrive…blood!

Hair
Hair
The men of "the tribe" have grown their hair long as a symbol of rebellion against authority. The proudly sing of their rebellious symbol.

Heart
Damn Yankees
Van Buren, manager for a loosing baseball team attempts to cheer up the team after another defeat.

Her Face
Carnival
Paul, an introverted and crippled puppeteer with the carnival at first denies his feelings for his new assistant Lili but then realizes he is in love.

Hey There
Pajama Game
Factory Supervisor Sid has fallen for Union Representative Babe who rejects him. Sid tries to talk himself out of being in love.

Highway Miles
The Flood
Raleigh, a teenager from small-town Meyerville, tells of his desire to leave, to see the world beyond his home.

Home
(*Michael Bublé*)
The singer, though happy to be living his dream, is far from those he loves and longs to return home.

How Lucky You Are
Seussical the Musical
The Cat in the Hat sings a satirical song to cheer up the constantly whining Mayzie, trying to get her to look at the good side of life.

Hushabye Mountain
Chitty Chitty Bang Bang
Caractacus Potts is a single father and magical but unsuccessful inventor. He sings a lullaby to his two children.

I Can See It
The Fantasticks
Mathew, although in love with Luisa, is curious to see the world and experience adventure. He abandons Luisa to follow his worldly dreams.

I Can't Be Bothered Now
Crazy for You
Bobby is a young banker who'd rather be in show business. As his mother and fiancée nag him about his future, Bobby dreams he's performing in a musical.

I Could Write a Book
Pal Joey
Joey is a charming nightclub performer and womanizer. He meets the naïve Linda and begins to charm her with his tried and true pick-up line.

I Love to Rhyme
Goldwyn Follies (1938)
The singer shows off his love of rhyming and uses it to charm the girl.

I Married an Angel
I Married an Angel
The gods send an angel down to marry the vain banker Willie Palaffi and teach him a lesson. Willie brags about his new wife.

I Met a Girl
Bells are Ringing
Jeff, a playwright, meets the mysterious Ella who cures him of writer's block. Jeff realizes he's fallen in love and declares it to the world.

I Want to be Seen With You Tonight
Funny Girl
Ziegfeld Follies comedian Fanny Brice fascinates playboy/gambler Nick Arnstein. Knowing she's susceptible to his charms, he begins to woo her.

I Want to Make Magic
Fame: The Musical
Nick, a former child actor now attending a high school for the performing arts shares his dreams of being a serious actor with scene partner Serena.

I'd Rather Be Sailing
A New Brain
Roger sings of his passion and reasons for sailing.

I'm Alive
Next to Normal
The teenaged Gabe has been dead for 16 years, yet continues to haunt his mother's mind insisting she not forget him. He's alive in her imagination.

I'm Calm
A Funny Thing Happened on the Way to the Forum
Hysterium, head slave in the house of Senex, is easily upset. He tries to calm himself.

I'm Not That Smart
The 25th Annual Putnam County Spelling Bee
Leaf Conybear's family constantly tells Leaf how stupid he is. Through his success at spelling, Leaf realizes they are wrong.

I've Got Beginner's Luck
Shall We Dance (1937 film)
Peter, a ballet dancer has fallen in love with Linda, a tap dancer. Despite her rebuffing his affections, Peter decides to woo her.

I've Grown Accustomed to Her Face
My Fair Lady
Through his cold manners, Professor Higgins has driven his elocution pupil Eliza, from his home. He realizes his true feelings in her absence.

If Ever I Would Leave You
Camelot
In an effort to end their doomed love, Queen Guenevere attempts to send Lancelot away. Lancelot finds he cannot leave.

If I Only Had a Brain
The Wizard of Oz
Scarecrow tells Dorothy of his wish for a brain, listing all the wonderful things he would do and think if he had one.

If This Isn't Love
Finian's Rainbow
Woody has fallen in love with Irish lass Sharon. Excited, Woody's mute sister Susan wants to tell the world. Woody interprets.

If You Can Find Me, I'm Here
Evening Primrose
Sick of the world, Charles, a young poet seeks refuge by hiding out in a department store. He bids the world goodbye.

In a Little While
Once Upon a Mattress
Sir Harry is off in search of a bride for Prince Dauntless. He calms his anxious sweetheart saying that they too soon will marry.

Into the Fire
The Scarlet Pimpernel
Sir Percy rallies his comrades to go to France and save the lives of innocent people threatened by execution at the guillotine.

It's Got to be Love
On Your Toes
Junior, a college music teacher and former vaudeville performer, sings (and dances) to a new song written by his pupil.

It's No Problem
High Fidelity
Tired of being bullied by his co-worker, Dick, a mild mannered record store clerk finally stands his ground, defending his new girlfriend.

It's Not All Right
Striking 12
After reading "The Little Match Girl" and recognizing his hypocrisy, a grumpy man decides to change his ways.

It's Possible
Seussical the Musical
During his evening bath, Jojo lets his imagination go, making up creative "thinks." This sends Jojo on a magical journey of limitless possibilities.

Just In Time
Bells are Ringing
Through Ella's encouragement, Jeff finishes his play. Jeff tells Ella that her love has saved him.

Ladies' Choice
Hairspray — The Movie
Teen heartthrob Link Larkin performs this flirtatious number for live television broadcast of a local high school dance.

Larger Than Life
My Favorite Year
Benjy, a young TV comedy writer explains his excitement for an upcoming guest star actor and the important role this actor played in Benjy's childhood.

Last One Picked
Howard Crabtree's Whoop-dee-doo!
The singer recounts the awkward school days when he was a total failure at gym class.

Lay All Your Love on Me
Mamma Mia!
Sky tries to cheer up his confused fiancée Sophie by promising he will always be the one man there for her.

Left Behind
Spring Awakening
At the funeral for his friend, teenaged Melchior questions the parents as to why they pushed their son to the point of taking his own life.

Let's Do It, Let's Fall in Love
Paris
Guy Pennel, French actor and leading man flirts with his scene partner despite her engagement to an American.

Lily's Eyes
The Secret Garden
Archibald has taken on the guardianship of his orphaned niece. But the girl troubles him as she shares the same features as his deceased wife, Lily.

Lonesome Polecat
Seven Brides for Seven Brothers
Seven brothers, all ranchers, pine for the girls they met at a town festival.

Love, I Hear
A Funny Thing Happened on the Way to the Forum
The naïve Hero questions the strange feelings he's having in regards to the girl next door.

Lucky to be Me
On the Town
Gabey, a sailor on leave in Manhattan, has been searching for the beautiful girl he saw on a poster. What luck! He finds her and she agrees to go on a date with him.

Mister Cellophane
Chicago
Amos, the husband of famed murderess Roxie Hart, sings (apologetically) of his frustration in being treated like he's invisible – like cellophane.

My Unfortunate Erection (Chip's Lament)
The 25th Annual Putnam County Spelling Bee
A pretty girl in the audience distracts Chip, the winner of last year's Spelling Bee. He misspells a word and is eliminated. Frustrated, Chip sings.

New York, New York
On the Town
Three sailors are on leave in New York Excited, they wish to see the entire city in one day.

The Night That Goldman Spoke
Ragtime
Younger Brother is searching for meaning in his life. Overhearing political activist Emma Goldman speak about social justice for the lower classes, he finds his cause.

On the Street Where You Live
My Fair Lady
Freddy is infatuated with Eliza who resides at Professor Higgins' home. He strolls up and down her street hoping to see her.

Perfect for You
Next to Normal
Natalie rejects Henry's affections stating how messed-up she is. Henry professes his love stating he's not a perfect guy – therefore absolutely perfect for her.

The Proposal
Titanic: A New Musical
Barrett, a stoker on the Titanic, sends a wireless telegraph to his sweetheart – a marriage proposal for when he returns.

The Rain Song
110 in the Shade
Starbuck, a drifter and con man arrives in a town plagued by a drought. He convinces the citizens that he has magic powers to conjure up rain – for a small fee.

Razzle Dazzle
Chicago
Unscrupulous lawyer Billy Flynn explains his successful strategy at winning court cases – not by presenting the truth, but by putting on a show.

Run Away With Me
The Unauthorized Autobiography of Samantha Brown
When teenaged Samantha finds herself at a crossroads in life, her high school sweetheart Adam offers his vision of their future.

Sandy
Grease
Angered by his inappropriate passes, Sandy abandons Danny at the drive-in. Only then does Danny realize how much Sandy means to him.

Singin' in the Rain
Singin' in the Rain
Don Lockwood has fallen in love with Kathy Sheldon. After escorting her home and kissing her goodnight, he walks home hardly noticing the pouring rain.

Slide Some Oil to Me
The Wiz
The rusted Tin Man begs Dorothy to grease his joints so he can move again.

Song of Love
Once Upon a Mattress
Prince Dauntless proclaims his love of Princess Winifred of the swamps – a very unusual girl and one greatly disapproved of by his mother the Queen.

Streets of Dublin
A Man of No Importance
Alfie lives his life buried in the literature of Oscar Wilde. Young Robbie shows Alfie the poetry of Robbie's world – the living characters on the streets of Dublin.

Suddenly Seymour
Little Shop of Horrors
Seymour and Audrey confess their feelings for one another and Seymour vows to always protect and take care of Audrey.

Take a Chance on Me
Little Women
Laurie lives an isolated life jealously watching the March sisters having fun next door. At a dance, he asks Jo March to be his friend.

Tell My Father
The Civil War
Private Sam Taylor pens a letter to home before going into battle.

There Once Was a Man
Pajama Game
Sid is in love with Babe. He describes how his love is bigger than all the love stories that have ever gone before.

They Can't Take That Away from Me
Crazy for You
Bobby's efforts to save Polly's theater have failed. Saying goodbye, he hints at his feelings, hoping Polly will ask him to stay.

They Were You
The Fantasticks
After learning many hard lessons about life, Mathew returns home to his sweetheart Luisa knowing that true happiness is with her.

Those Were the Good Old Days
Damn Yankees
Applegate (the Devil) is disenchanted by the world as of late – too many honest and sincere people. He muses on the evil days gone by.

Too Darn Hot
Kiss Me Kate
During an intermission break, the dancer Paul muses about the weather interfering with his after show plans.

Wait Till We're Sixty-Five
On a Clear Day You Can See Forever
Conservative college student Warren excitedly tells his fiancée Daisy about the secure future life he has planned out for them.

What am I Doin'?
Closer Than Ever
The singer remembers his crazy actions of when he first fell in love.

What Do I Need With Love
Thoroughly Modern Millie
Jimmy, a confirmed bachelor meets Millie, a carefree girl. Fascinated, Jimmy fights to keep his feelings in check. He loses.

What Would I Do If I Could Feel?
The Wiz
Tin Man pleads with The Wizard for a heart.

The Wheels of a Dream
Ragtime
Ragtime pianist Coalhouse Walker tells of his dreams for his family's future and of his belief that in America, he can achieve these dreams despite race or social status.

When I Get My Name in Lights
The Boy from Oz
Young Peter dances and sings every chance he gets, hoping to be noticed and make it in show biz.

When I'm Not Near the Girl I Love
Finian's Rainbow
The Leprechaun Og is turning mortal. He is having mortal feelings he can't control – like endlessly falling in love.

Where Do I Go?
Hair
Confused and caught between society's expectations and the beliefs of his hippie tribe, Claude wonders about his own path in life.

Who I'd Be
Shrek: The Musical
Confiding in Donkey, Shrek tells of his dreams – what he'd do and who he'd be if he weren't an ogre.

Winter's on the Wing
The Secret Garden
Dickson, a boy with a mysterious connection to nature, calls forth spring.

With You
Pippin
Pippin involves himself with a string of different girls, and wonders if lighthearted relationships are the secret to happiness.

You Are My Home
The Scarlet Pimpernel
Armand, a member of the Scarlet Pimpernel's secret league is leaving to go to France to save innocent lives from the guillotine. His sister Marguerite begs him to stay.

You Mustn't Kick it Around
Pal Joey (film)
Joey, a cad and club entertainer sings a number about love being "kicked" around by a callous lover – something he does to others regularly.

You're Getting to Be a Habit With Me
42nd Street
A standard sung by Frank Sinatra, Frankie Avalon, Doris Day. Used as a production number in 42nd Street.

Song Indexes

Vocal Styles

Some songs, especially early standards, may be sung with different vocal styles or in a combination of styles depending on acting intent. These will be listed in more than one category.

LEGIT

All I Need is the Girl
Bring Me My Bride
Brush Up Your Shakespeare
C'est Moi
Come Back to Me
Dames
Easy to Love
Evenin' Star
Everybody Says Don't
Fit as a Fiddle (and Ready for Love)
Heart
Her Face
Hey There
Hushabye Mountain
I Can See It
I Can't Be Bothered Now
I Could Write a Book
I Love to Rhyme
I Married an Angel
I Met a Girl
I Want to be Seen With You Tonight
I'm Calm
I've Got Beginner's Luck
I've Grown Accustomed to Her Face
If Ever I Would Leave You
If I Only Had a Brain
If This Isn't Love
It's Got to Be Love
Just in Time
Lucky to be Me
Love, I Hear
Let's Do It, Let's Fall in Love
New York, New York
On the Street Where You Live
The Proposal
The Rain Song
Razzle Dazzle
Singin' in the Rain
Song of Love
There Once was a Man
They Can't Take That Away From Me
They Were You
Those Were the Good Old Days
Wait Till We're Sixty-Five
The Wheels of a Dream
When I'm Not Near the Girl I Love
With You
You Mustn't Kick it Around
You're Getting to be a Habit with Me

BELT

21 Guns
All I Care About is Love
And They're Off
Brush Up Your Shakespeare
Come Back to Me
Corner of the Sky
Different
Desperado
Everybody Says Don't
Grow For Me
Hair
Heart
Highway Miles
I Can See It
I Met a Girl
I'd Rather be Sailing
I'm Alive
I'm Not that Smart
If You Can Find Me I'm Here
Into the Fire
It's No Problem
Ladies' Choice
Last One Picked
Lay All Your Love on Me
Lily's Eyes
Mister Cellophane
My Unfortunate Erection (Chip's Lament)
New York, New York
The Night That Goldman Spoke
The Rain Song
Slide Some Oil to Me
The Streets of Dublin

Suddenly Seymour
Take a Chance on Me
There Once was a Man
Those Were the Good Old Days
Too Darn Hot
What am I Doin'?
What Do I Need with Love
What Would I Do If I Could Feel?
When I Get My Name in Lights
Who I'd Be
Winter's on the Wing
You are My Home

MIX
All I Care About is Love
All I Need is the Girl
All That's Known
Alone in the Universe
Boulevard of Broken Dreams
Different
Desperado
Home
How Lucky You Are
I Want to Make Magic
I'd Rather be Sailing
It's No Problem
It's Not All Right
It's Possible (In McElligot's Pool)
Larger Than Life
Lay All Your Love on Me
Left Behind
Perfect for You
The Proposal
Sandy
Slide Some Oil to Me
Tell My Father
What Would I Do If I Could Feel?
Where Do I Go?
Who I'd Be
Winter's on the Wing
With You

Comedy/Dramatic

DRAMATIC
21 Guns
All That's Known
Alone in the Universe
Boulevard of Broken Dreams
Come Back to Me
Corner of the Sky
Different
Desperado
Evenin' Star
Everybody Says Don't
Hair
Her Face
Hey There
Highway Miles
Home
Hushabye Mountain
I Can See It
I Want to be Seen With You Tonight
I Want to Make Magic
I'd Rather be Sailing
I'm Alive
I've Grown Accustomed to Her Face
If Ever I Would Leave You
If You Can Find Me I'm Here
Into the Fire
It's Not All Right
It's Possible (In McElligot's Pool)
Larger Than Life
Left Behind
Lily's Eyes
Lucky to be Me
Mister Cellophane
The Night That Goldman Spoke
On the Street Where You Live
Perfect for You
The Proposal
The Rain Song
The Streets of Dublin
Take a Chance on Me
Tell My Father
They Can't Take That Away From Me
They Were You
What am I Doin'?
What Would I Do If I Could Feel?
The Wheels of a Dream
Where Do I Go?
Who I'd Be
With You
Winter's on the Wing
You are My Home

COMEDIC

All I Care About is Love
All I Need is the Girl
And They're Off
Bring Me My Bride
Brush Up Your Shakespeare
C'est Moi
Dames
Easy to Love
Fit as a Fiddle (and Ready for Love)
Grow For Me
Heart
How Lucky You Are
I Can't Be Bothered Now
I Could Write a Book
I Love to Rhyme
I Married an Angel
I Met a Girl
I'm Calm
I'm Not that Smart
I've Got Beginner's Luck
If I Only Had a Brain
If This Isn't Love
It's Got to Be Love
It's No Problem
Just in Time
Ladies' Choice
Last One Picked
Lay All Your Love on Me
Let's Do It, Let's Fall in Love
Love, I Hear
My Unfortunate Erection (Chip's Lament)
New York, New York
Razzle Dazzle
Sandy
Singin' in the Rain
Slice Some Oil to Me
Song of Love
Suddenly Seymour
There Once was a Man
Those Were the Good Old Days
Too Darn Hot
Wait Till We're Sixty-Five
What Do I Need with Love
When I Get My Name in Lights
When I'm Not Near the Girl I Love
You Mustn't Kick it Around
You're Getting to be a Habit with Me

Historical Category

Standard, Golden Age, Contemporary, Pop/Rock

STANDARD

Dames
Easy to Love
Fit as a Fiddle (and Ready for Love)
I Can't Be Bothered Now
I Could Write a Book
I Love to Rhyme
I Married an Angel
I've Got Beginner's Luck
It's Got to Be Love
Let's Do It, Let's Fall in Love
Singin' in the Rain
They Can't Take That Away From Me
You Mustn't Kick it Around
You're Getting to be a Habit with Me

GOLDEN AGE

All I Need is the Girl
Bring Me My Bride
Brush Up Your Shakespeare
C'est Moi
Come Back to Me
Corner of the Sky
Evenin' Star
Everybody Says Don't
Heart
Her Face
Hey There
Hushabye Mountain
I Can See It
I Met a Girl
I Want to be Seen With You Tonight
I'm Calm
I've Grown Accustomed to Her Face
If Ever I Would Leave You
If I Only Had a Brain
If This Isn't Love
If You Can Find Me I'm Here
Just in Time
Love, I Hear
Lucky to be Me
Mister Cellophane
New York, New York
On the Street Where You Live
The Rain Song

Razzle Dazzle
Song of Love
There Once Was a Man
They Were You
Those Were the Good Old Days
Too Darn Hot
Wait Till We're Sixty-Five
When I'm Not Near the Girl I Love
With You

CONTEMPORARY

21 Guns
All I Care About is Love
All That's Known
Alone in the Universe
And They're Off
Different
Grow For Me
Hair
Highway Miles
How Lucky You Are
I Want to Make Magic
I'd Rather be Sailing
I'm Alive
I'm Not that Smart
Into the Fire
It's No Problem
It's Not All Right
It's Possible (In McElligot's Pool)
Ladies' Choice
Larger Than Life
Last One Picked
Left Behind
Lily's Eyes
My Unfortunate Erection (Chips' Lament)
The Night That Goldman Spoke
Perfect for You
The Proposal
Sandy
Slide Some Oil to Me
The Streets of Dublin
Suddenly Seymour
Take a Chance on Me
Tell My Father
What am I Doin'?
What Do I Need with Love
What Would I Do If I Could Feel?
The Wheels of a Dream
When I Get My Name in Lights
Where Do I Go?
Who I'd Be
Winter's on the Wing
You are My Home

POP/ROCK

21 Guns
Boulevard of Broken Dreams
Desperado
Hair
Highway Miles
Home
I'm Alive
It's Not All Right
Lay All Your Love on Me
Perfect for You
Sandy
Slide Some Oil to Me
Suddenly Seymour
What Would I Do If I Could Feel?
Where Do I Go?
Who I'd Be

Timeline

Songs are listed by the year they were composed. If used in a later production, the additional year is listed in parenthesis.

1928 Fit as a Fiddle (and Ready for Love) (1955)
1928 Singin' in the Rain (1955)
1928 Let's Do It, Let's Fall in Love
1932 You're Getting to be a Habit With Me
1933 Dames (1980)
1936 Easy to Love
1936 It's Got to be Love
1937 I Can't Be Bothered Now (1992)
1937 I've Got Beginner's Luck
1937 They Can't Take That Away from Me
1938 I Love to Rhyme
1938 I Married an Angel
1939 If I Only Had a Brain
1940 I Could Write a Book
1940 You Mustn't Kick it Around
1944 Lucky to Be Me
1944 New York, New York
1947 If This Isn't Love
1947 When I'm Not Near the Girl I Love
1948 Brush Up Your Shakespeare
1948 Too Darn Hot
1954 Hey There
1954 Lonesome Polecat
1954 There Once was a Man
1955 Heart
1955 Those Were the Good Ole' Days
1956 I Met a Girl
1956 Just in Time
1959 All I Need is the Girl
1959 In a Little While
1959 Song of Love
1960 C'est Moi
1960 I Can See It
1960 If Ever I Would Leave You
1960 They Were You
1961 Her Face
1962 Bring Me My Bride
1962 I'm Calm
1962 Love, I Hear
1963 Evenin' Star
1963 The Rain Song
1964 Everybody Says Don't
1964 I Want to Be Seen With You Tonight
1964 I've Grown Accustomed to Her Face
1964 On the Street Where You Live
1965 Come Back to Me
1965 Wait Till We're Sixty-Five
1966 If You Can Find Me I'm Here
1968 Hair
1968 Hushabye Mountain
1968 Where Do I Go?
1972 Corner of the Sky
1972 With You
1973 Desperado
1975 All I Care About is Love
1975 Mister Cellophane
1975 Razzle Dazzle
1975 Slide Some Oil to Me
1975 What Would I Do If I Could Feel?
1978 Sandy
1981 Lay All Your Love On Me (2001)
1982 Grow for Me
1982 Suddenly Seymour
1988 I Want to Make Magic
1989 What am I Doin'?
1989 When I Get My Name in Lights (1998)
1991 Lily's Eyes
1991 Winter's on the Wing
1992 Larger Than Life
1993 Different
1993 Last One Picked
1997 Into the Fire
1997 You Are My Home
1997 The Proposal
1998 And They're Off
1998 I'd Rather Be Sailing
1998 The Night that Goldman Spoke
1998 The Wheels of a Dream
1999 Tell My Father
2000 Alone in the Universe
2000 How Lucky You Are
2000 It's Possible (In McElligot's Pool)
2001 Highway Miles
2002 Streets of Dublin
2002 What Do I Need with Love
2005 Home
2005 I'm Not that Smart
2005 My Unfortunate Erection
2005 Take a Chance on Me
2006 It's No Problem
2006 It's Not All Right
2007 Ladies' Choice
2008 All That's Known
2008 Left Behind
2008 Who I'd Be
2009 I'm Alive
2009 Perfect for You
2009 Run Away With Me
2010 21 Guns
2010 Boulevard of Broken Dreams

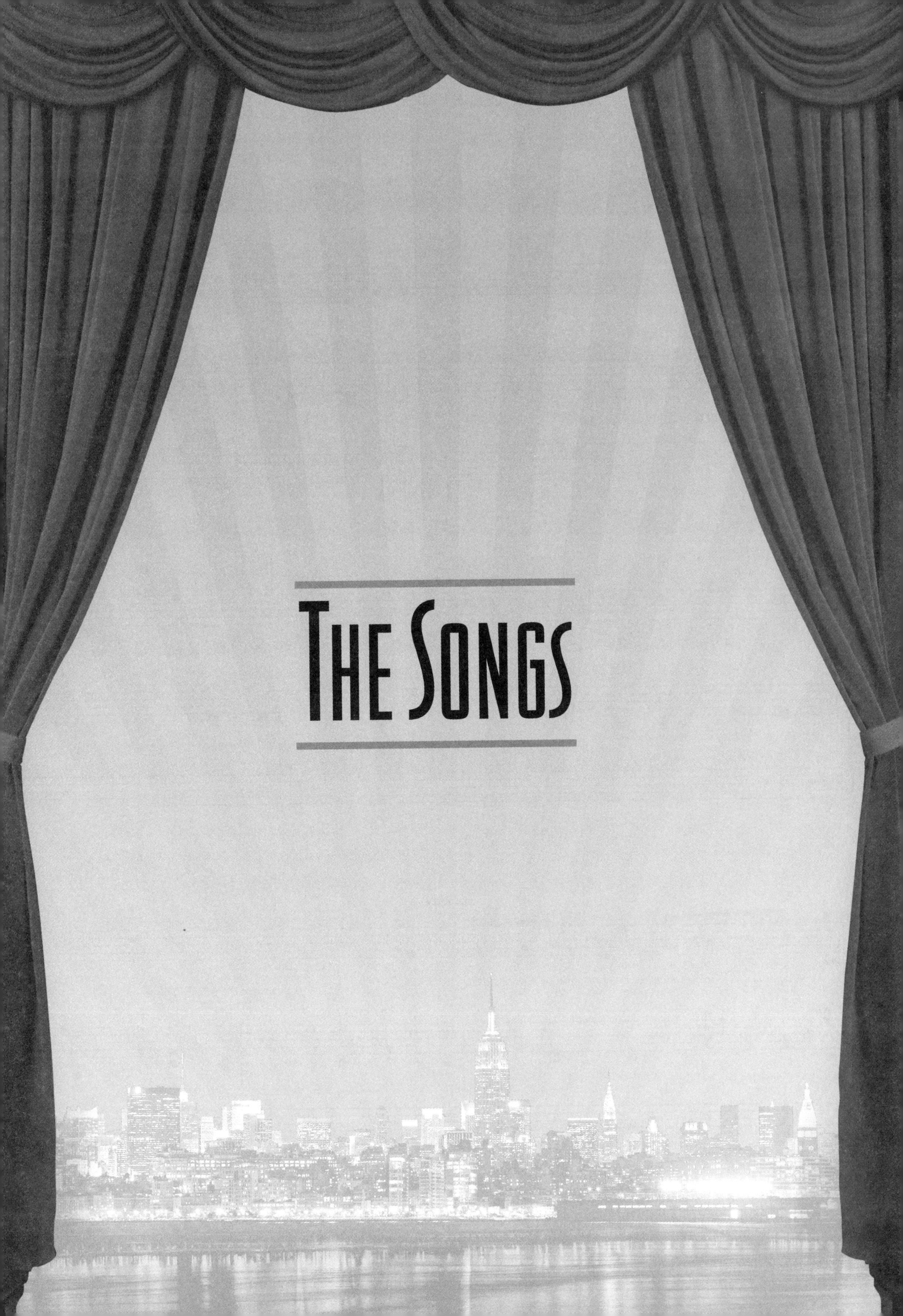

The Songs

21 GUNS

(from "American Idiot: The Musical")

Lyrics by
BILLIE JOE ARMSTRONG

Music by GREEN DAY
Arranged by TOM KITT

CD/TRACK 1/1

Medium pop/punk rock (♩ = 82)

11
F5
Am/E
Dm
F/C
B♭
F
One, twen - ty - one guns, lay down your arms, give up the fight.
f
14
C
F5
Am/E
Dm
F/C
One, twen - ty - one guns, throw up your arms
17
B♭
F
C
B♭5
F
in - to the sky, you and I.

ALL I CARE ABOUT IS LOVE

(from "Chicago")

Words by
FRED EBB

Music by
JOHN KANDER

CD/TRACK 1/2

Moderately (♩. = 100)

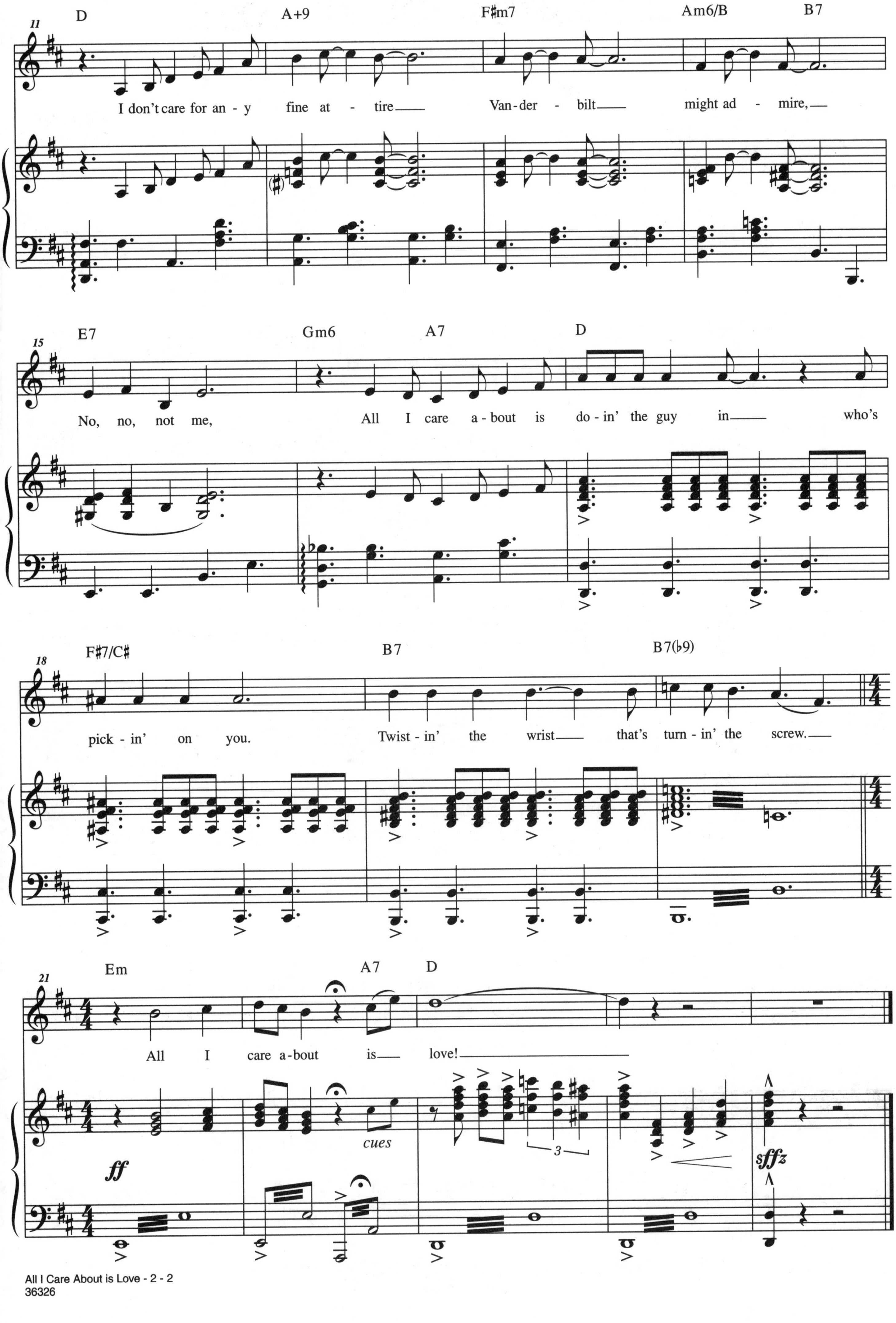
11
D
A+9
F♯m7
Am6/B
B7
I don't care for an - y fine at - tire
Van - der - bilt might ad - mire,
15
E7
Gm6
A7
D
No, no, not me,
All I care a - bout is do - in' the guy in who's
18
F♯7/C♯
B7
B7(♭9)
pick - in' on you.
Twist - in' the wrist that's turn - in' the screw.
21
Em
A7
D
All I care a - bout is love!
ff
cues
3
sffz

ALL I NEED IS THE GIRL
(from "Gypsy")

Lyrics by
STEPHEN SONDHEIM

Music by
JULE STYNE

CD/TRACK 1/3

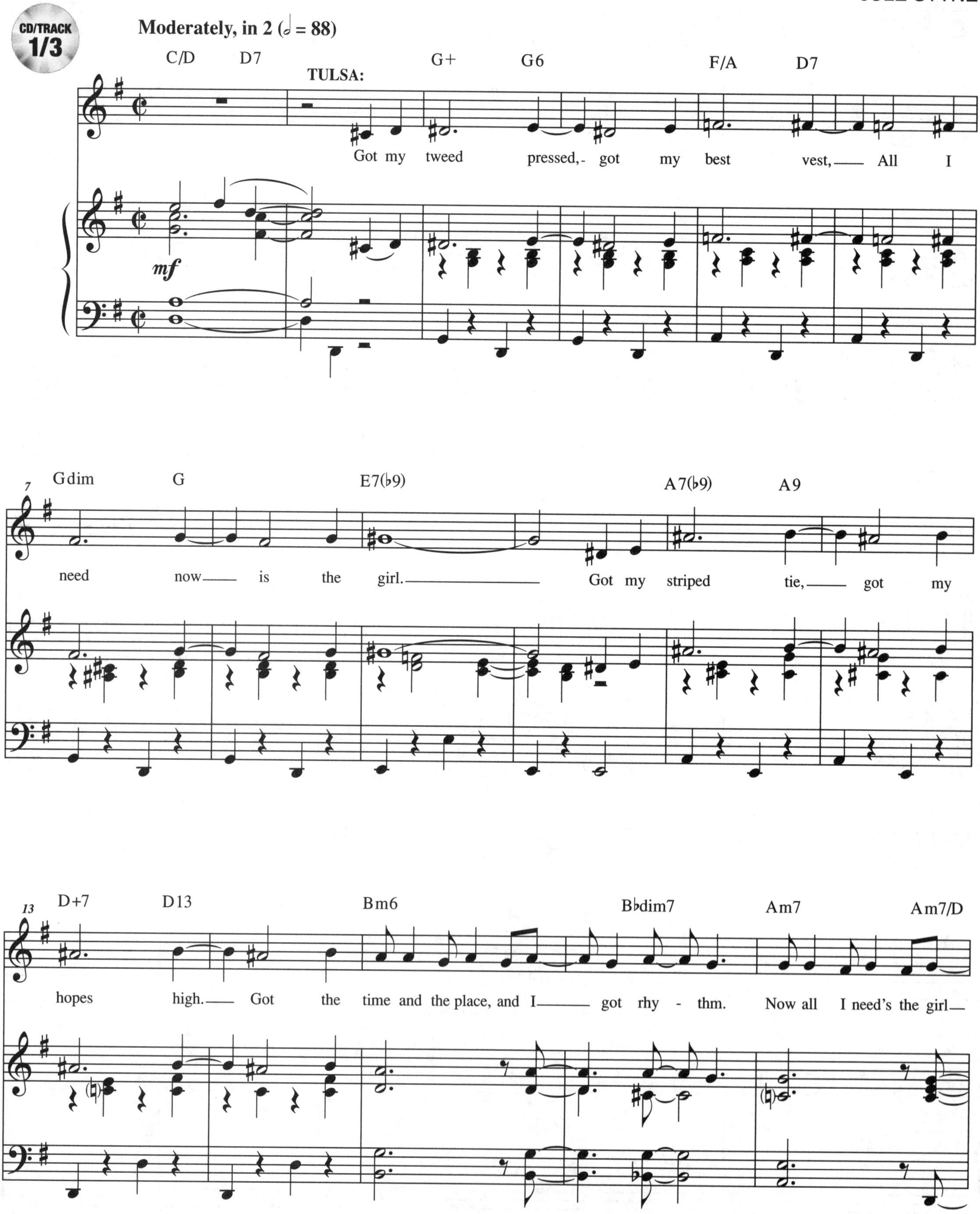

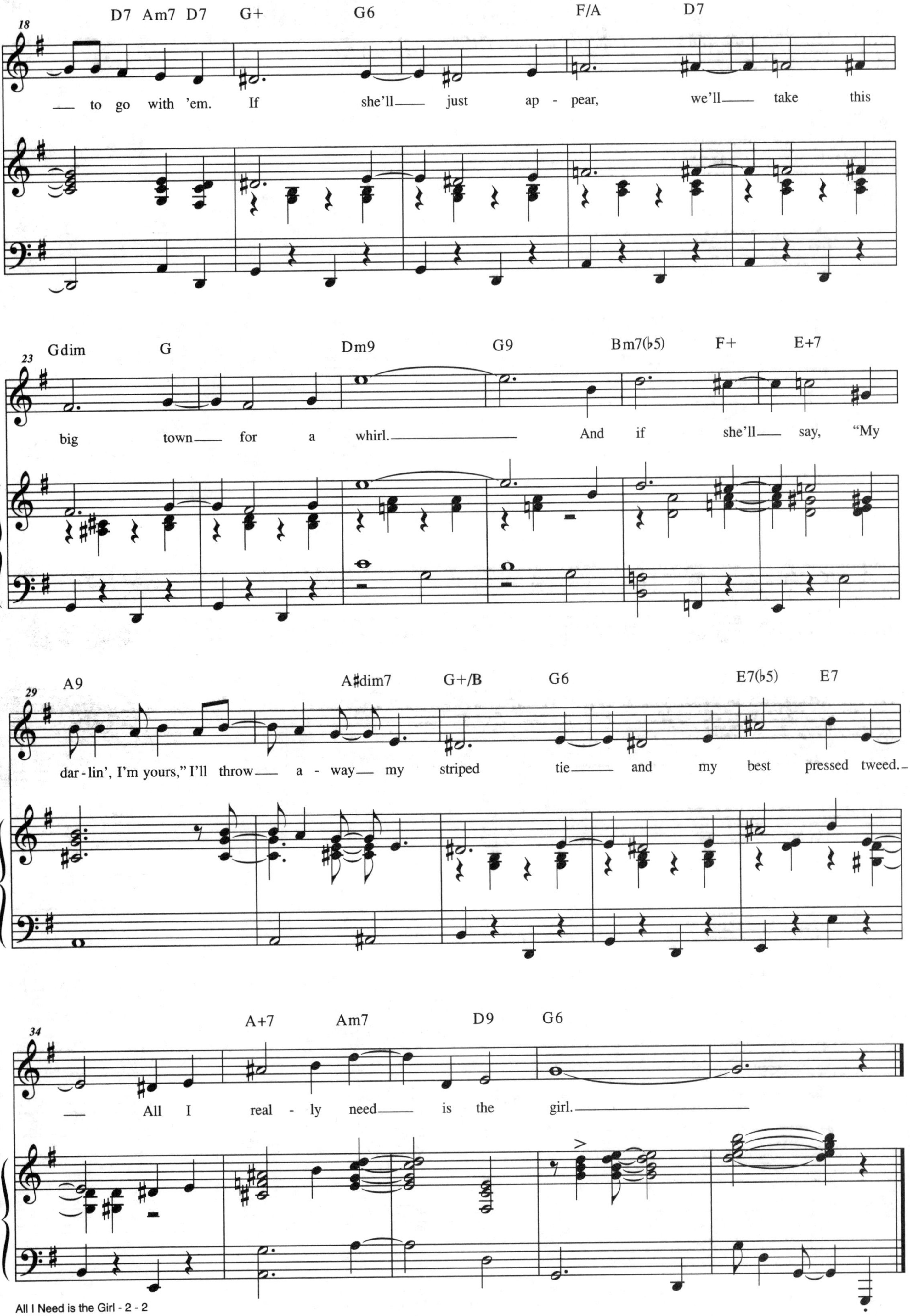
18
D7 Am7 D7 G+ G6 F/A D7
to go with 'em. If she'll just ap - pear, we'll take this
23
Gdim G Dm9 G9 Bm7(♭5) F+ E+7
big town for a whirl. And if she'll say, "My
29
A9 A♯dim7 G+/B G6 E7(♭5) E7
dar - lin', I'm yours," I'll throw a - way my striped tie and my best pressed tweed.
34
A+7 Am7 D9 G6
All I real - ly need is the girl.

ALL THAT'S KNOWN
(from "Spring Awakening")

Lyrics by
STEVEN SATER

Music by
DUNCAN SHEIK

10
C
B♭/D
B♭maj7
mf
— bad a - bout — you. —
But I know — there's so
mf
12
Am11
F11/E♭
3
much more to find, — just in look - ing through my - self and not at
14
Dm(add9)
B♭maj7
Am11
3
them.
Still I know — to trust my own true mind — and to
17
F11/E♭
3
Dm9/G
say — there's a way through — this.

ALONE IN THE UNIVERSE

(from "Seussical the Musical")

Lyrics by
LYNN AHRENS

Music by
STEPHEN FLAHERTY

CD/TRACK
1/5

With wonder (♩ = 96)

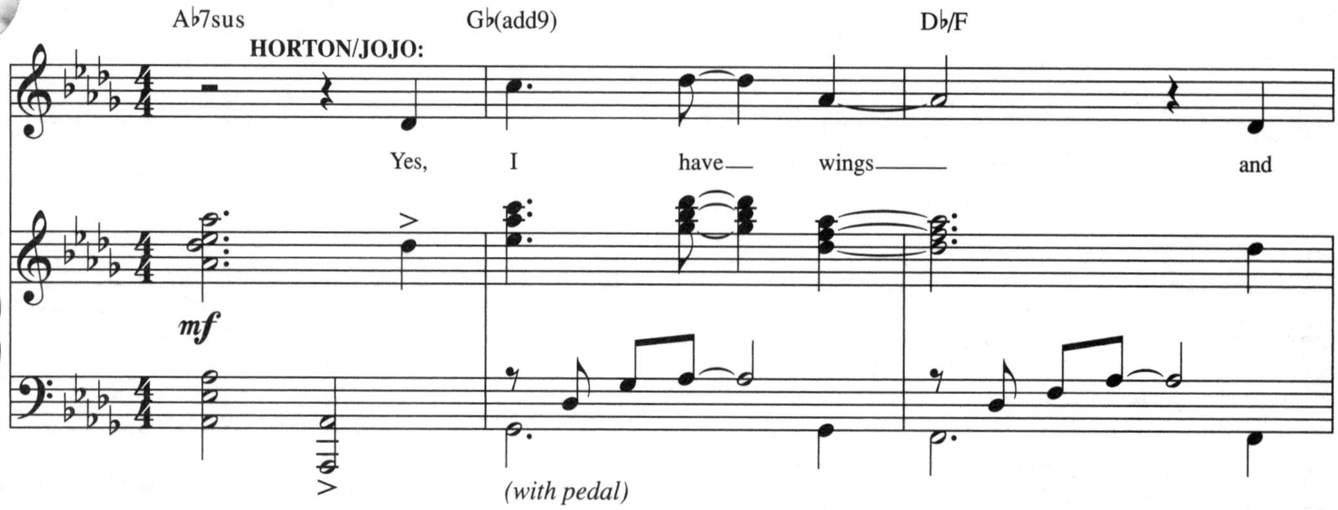

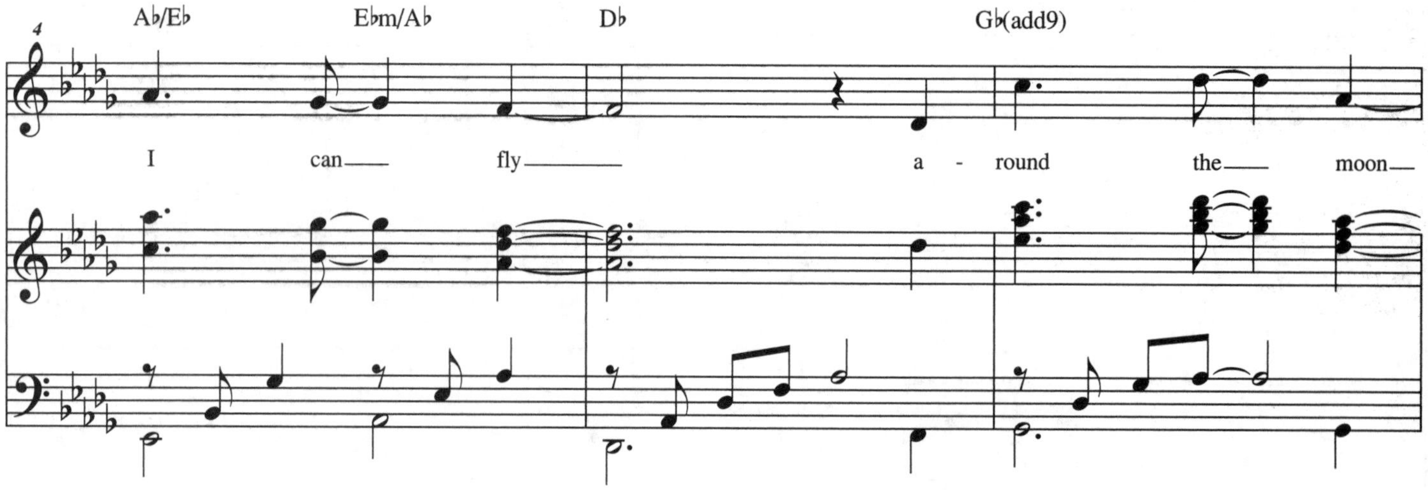

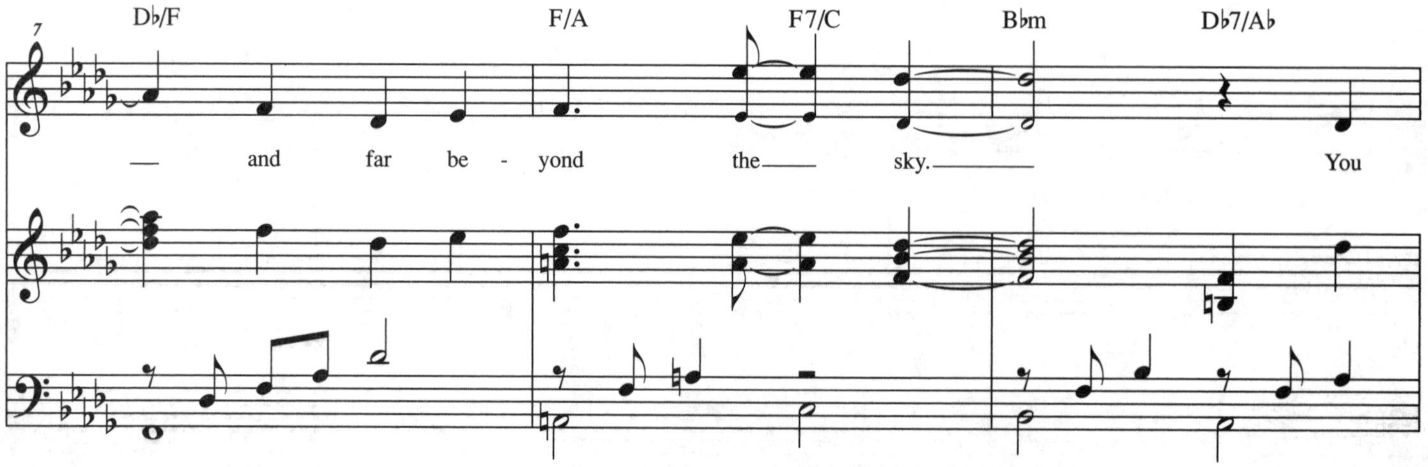

10
G♭(add9)
D♭/F
F♭
called my name and you set me free...
13
D♭/F
G♭(add9)
One small voice in the u - ni - verse...
mp
(with pedal)
16
D♭/F
B♭m11
E♭m11
A♭sus
One true friend in the u - ni - verse... who be -
(cues)
20
D♭(add9)
rit.
lieves in me.
rit.
pp

AND THEY'RE OFF

(from "A New Brain")

Words and Music by
WILLIAM FINN

CD/TRACK 1/6

In 4 (♩ = 144)
C Am G
off! Yeah, they're off.
F6/G C Am G
And they move in a herd, like a four letter word. And they're off.
E7/G♯ Am C9/G F D7/F♯
Tick-ets float to the ground. And the band
C/G G/A Am7 G F/G C
starts to play as the hors - es go 'round. And they're off!

BOULEVARD OF BROKEN DEAMS

(from "American Idiot: The Musical")

Words by
BILLIE JOE ARMSTRONG

Music by GREEN DAY
Arranged by TOM KITT

CD/TRACK 1/7

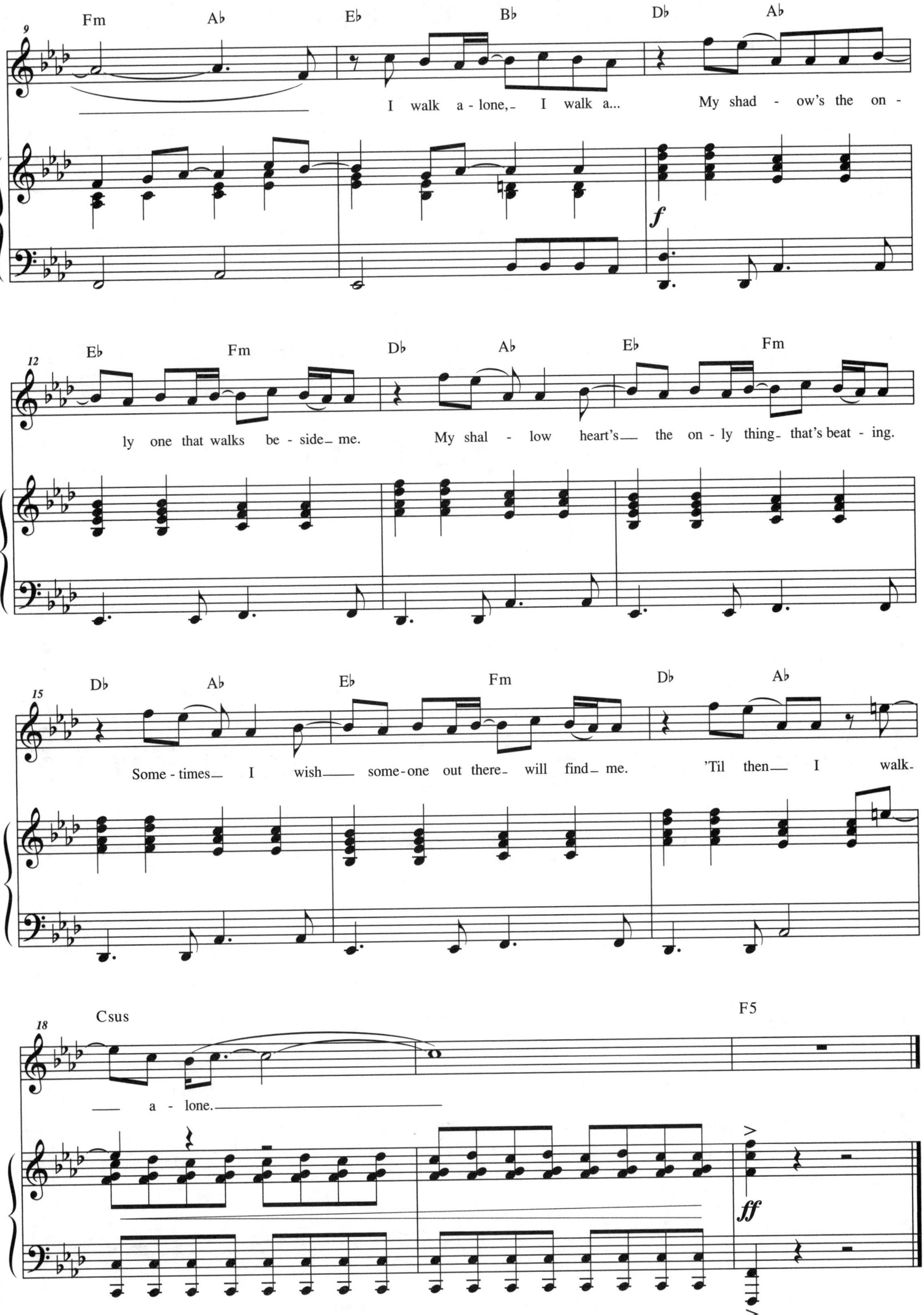
9
Fm Ab Eb Bb Db Ab
I walk a - lone, I walk a... My shad - ow's the on -
f
12
Eb Fm Db Ab Eb Fm
ly one that walks be - side me. My shal - low heart's the on - ly thing that's beat - ing.
15
Db Ab Eb Fm Db Ab
Some - times I wish some - one out there will find me. 'Til then I walk
18
Csus F5
a - lone.
ff

BRING ME MY BRIDE

(from "A Funny Thing Happened On the Way to the Forum")

Music and Lyrics by
STEPHEN SONDHEIM

CD/TRACK 1/8

Marciale (♩ = 112)

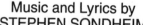

4x's
MILES:
mf
last time only
My bride! My bride! I've come to claim my bride. Come
ten - der-ly to crush her a-gainst my side! Let haste be made! I
can - not be de-layed! There are lands to con-quer, cit-ies to loot and peo - ple to de-grade! My

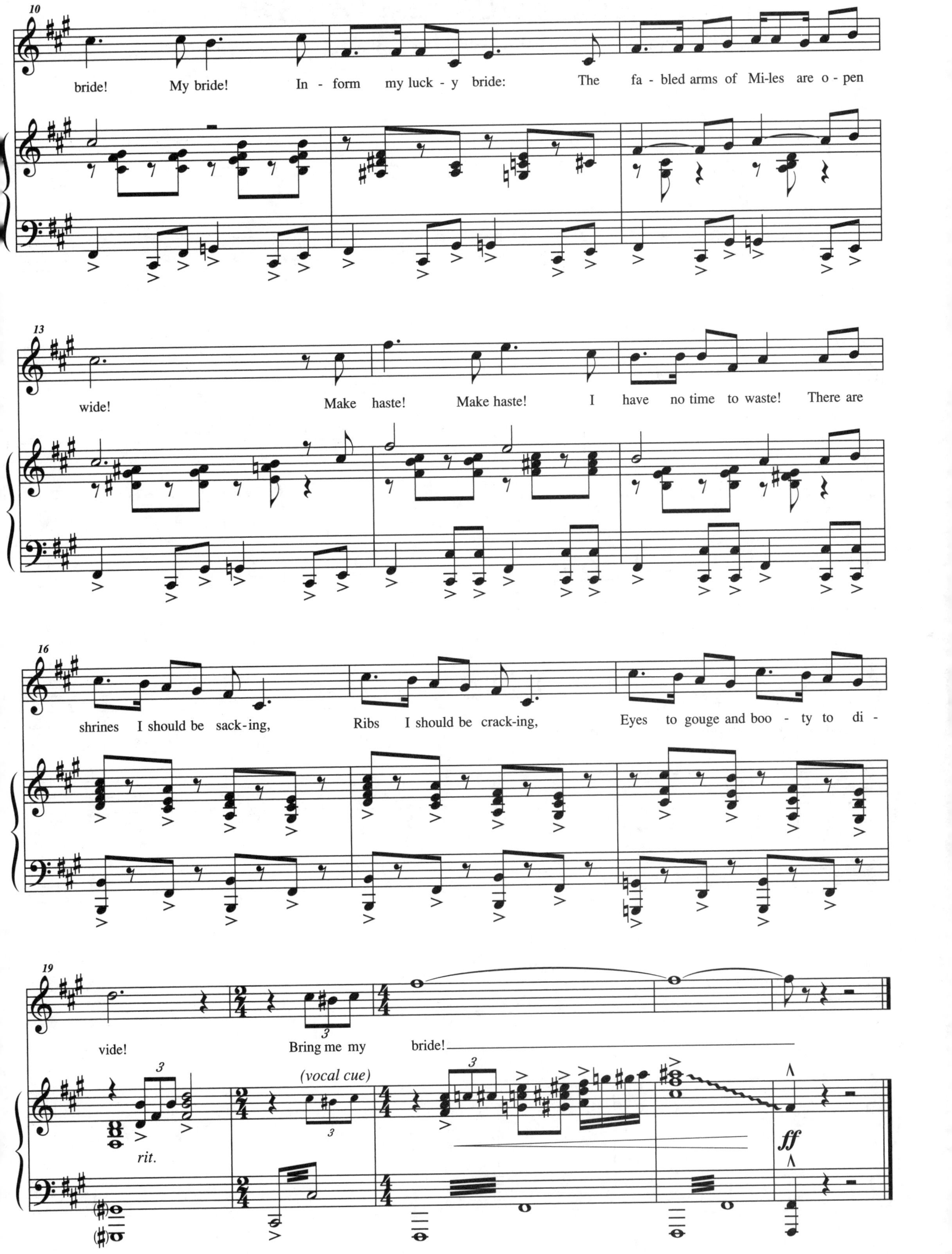
10
bride! My bride! In - form my luck - y bride: The fa - bled arms of Mi-les are o - pen
13
wide! Make haste! Make haste! I have no time to waste! There are
16
shrines I should be sack-ing, Ribs I should be crack-ing, Eyes to gouge and boo - ty to di -
19
vide! Bring me my bride!
(vocal cue)
rit.
ff

BRUSH UP YOUR SHAKESPEARE

(from "Kiss Me Kate")

Words and Music by
COLE PORTER

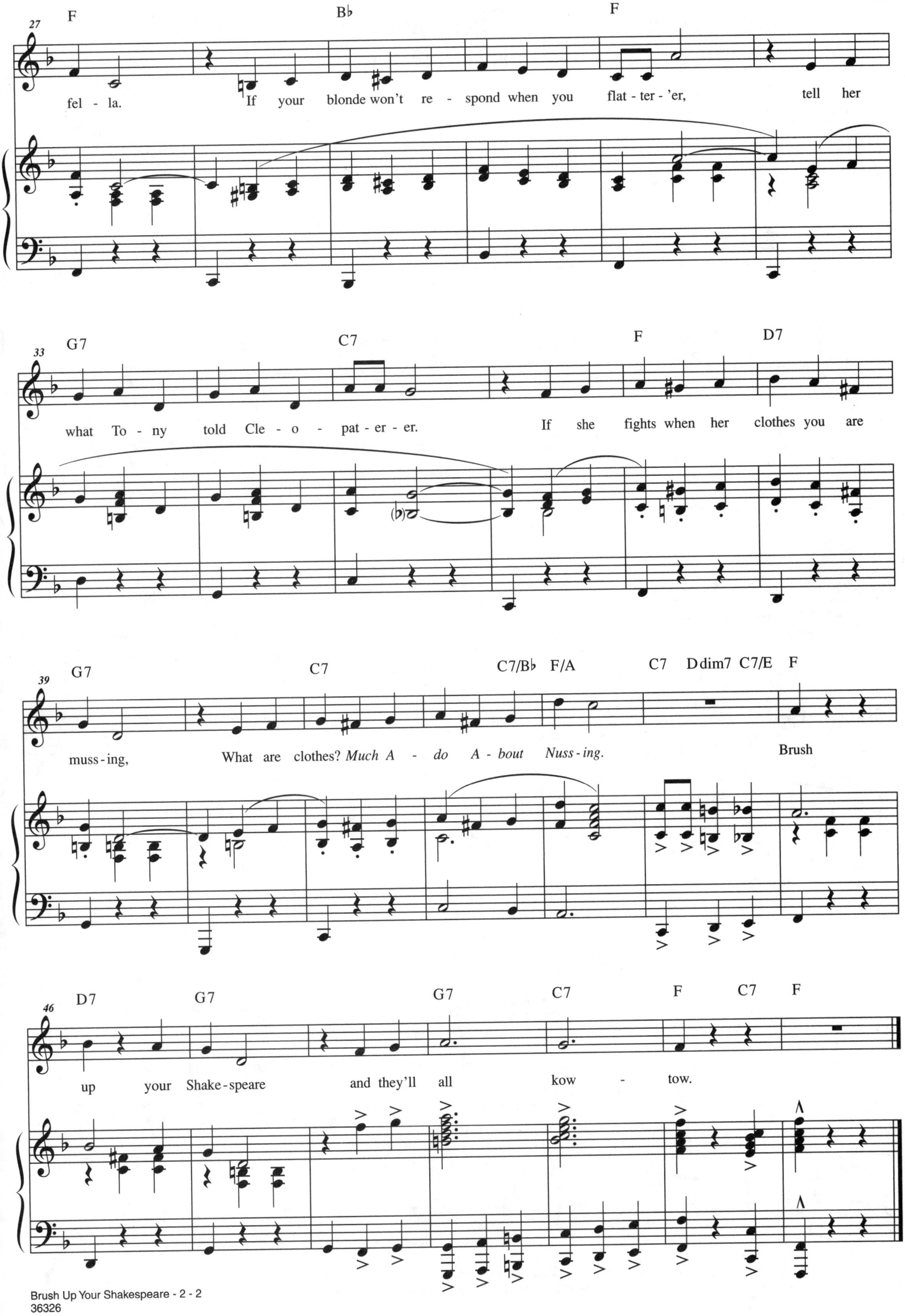
27
F Bb F
fel - la. If your blonde won't re - spond when you flat - ter - 'er, tell her
33
G7 C7 F D7
what To - ny told Cle - o - pat - er - er. If she fights when her clothes you are
39
G7 C7 C7/Bb F/A C7 Ddim7 C7/E F
muss - ing, What are clothes? Much A - do A - bout Nuss - ing. Brush
46
D7 G7 G7 C7 F C7 F
up your Shake - speare and they'll all kow - tow.

C'EST MOI
(from "Camelot")

Words by
ALAN JAY LERNER

Music by
FREDERICK LOEWE

CD/TRACK 1/10

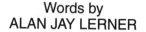

Allegretto scherzando (♩. = 76)
B♭/C C7 F C
LANCELOT:
I've ne - ver lost in
F C F C D7 Gm D7 Gm
bat - tle or game. I'm sim - ply the best by far. When
C F C D7 G7
swords are crossed 'tis al - ways the same, One blow and au re -

10
C7 F Am
voir! C'est moi! C'est moi! So
f
12
G7 C F Am G7 C
ad - m'rab - ly fit; A French Pro - me - theus un - bound. And
15
F Am B♭ F/A B♭ F/A
here I stand with val - or un - told, ex - cep - tion - 'ly brave, a -
18
B♭ F/C D7 Gm G7 C7 F C F
molto rit.
a tempo
maz - ing - ly bold, To serve at the Ta - ble Round! C'est moi!
molto rit.
a tempo

COME BACK TO ME

(from "On a Clear Day You Can See Forever")

Lyrics by
ALAN JAY LERNER

Music by
BURTON LANE

CD/TRACK 1/11

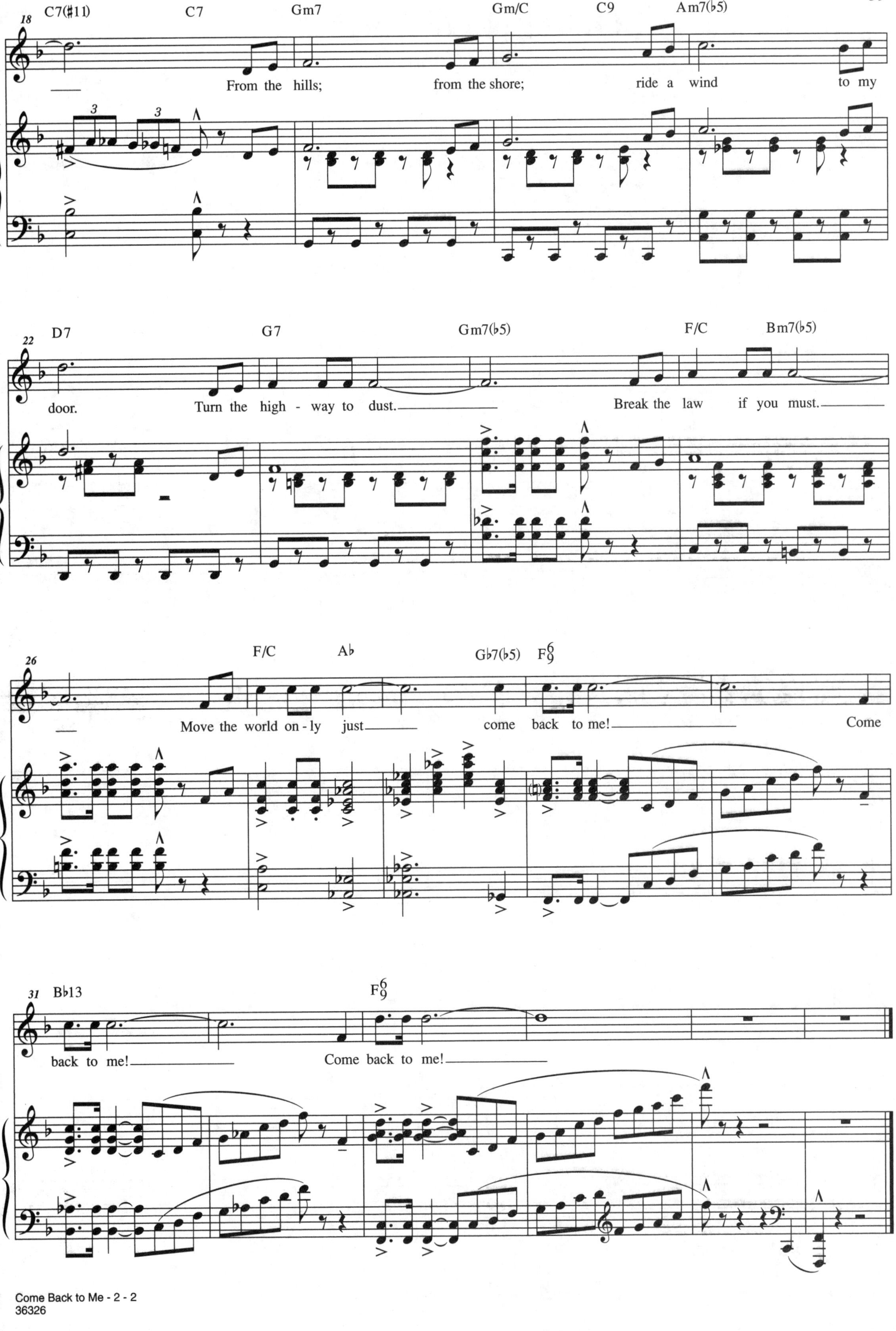
18
C7(♯11) C7 Gm7 Gm/C C9 Am7(♭5)
From the hills; from the shore; ride a wind to my
22
D7 G7 Gm7(♭5) F/C Bm7(♭5)
door. Turn the high - way to dust. Break the law if you must.
26
F/C A♭ G♭7(♭5) F6/9
Move the world on - ly just come back to me! Come
31
B♭13 F6/9
back to me! Come back to me!

CORNER OF THE SKY

(from "Pippin")

Words and Music by
STEPHEN SCHWARTZ

CD/TRACK 1/12

Slightly martial (♩ = 96)

12 Gsus G Em7 F
- ble, ea - gles be - long where they can fly;
15 C Dm/C G/B Am C/G F C/E Dm C
I've got to be where my spir-it can run free, got to find my cor - ner
18 Gm C Dm/C C Dm/C
of the sky.
21 C Dm/C C Dm/C C B♭/C F/A F C(add9)
rall.

DAMES
(from "42nd Street")

Words by
AL DUBIN

Music by
HARRY WARREN

CD/TRACK 1/13

Allegro, in 2 with a light bounce (𝅗𝅥 = 88)

11
F
Gm7
C7
F
But their ca - ress - es and home ad -
14
Gm7
C7
F6
B♭6
B♭m6
dress - es lin - ger in your mem - ry of those beau - ti - ful,
17
F6
B♭6
B♭m6
C6
in your mem - ry see those beau - ti - ful, in your mem - ry
20
C7sus/G
C9
F
Gm7/F
F
all those beau - ti - ful dames!
3
8va

DESPERADO

(recorded by The Eagles on their album "Desperado")

Words and Music by
DON HENLEY and GLENN FREY

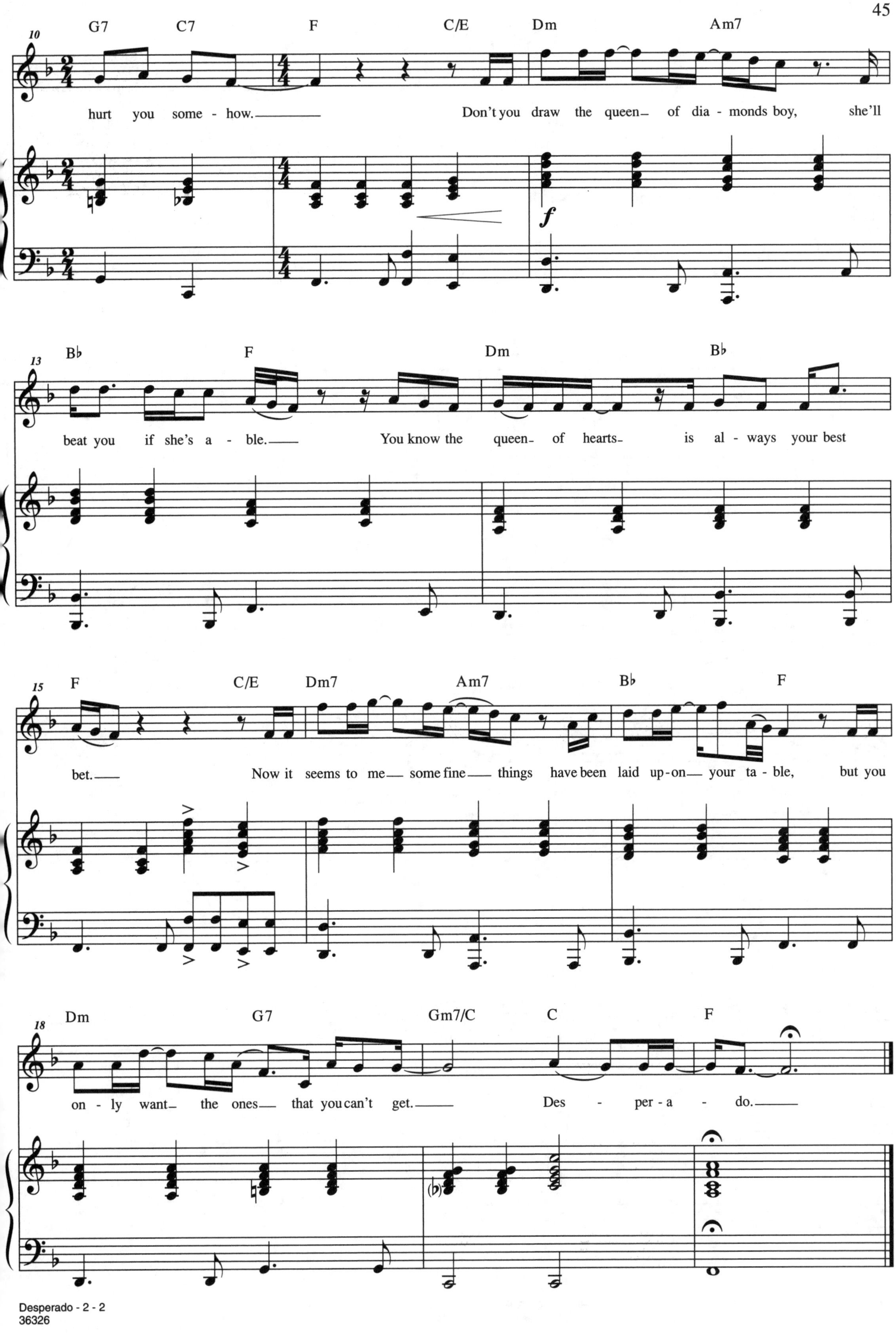
10
G7 C7 F C/E Dm Am7
hurt you some - how.
Don't you draw the queen of dia - monds boy, she'll
f
13
B♭ F Dm B♭
beat you if she's a - ble.
You know the queen of hearts is al - ways your best
15
F C/E Dm7 Am7 B♭ F
bet.
Now it seems to me some fine things have been laid up-on your ta - ble, but you
18
Dm G7 Gm7/C C F
on - ly want the ones that you can't get.
Des - per - a - do.

DIFFERENT

(from "Honk!")

Words by
ANTHONY DREWE

Music by
GEORGE STILES

CD/TRACK 1/15

Eb/F Dm/F Cm7 Eb/F Bb(add9)
a tempo
rall.
a tempo
e - go takes a knock. I'm just dif - ferent, but I
Ebmaj7
have a sense of pride. My looks may well be fun-ny but I hurt the same in - side.
Slowly
Gm7 Gm6 Cm7
Dif-ferent is - n't hate - ful, dif - ferent could be swell. Dif - ferent is just,
p
F+7 Bb(add9) Ebmaj7 Bb(add9)
rit.
well.... dif - ferent.

EASY TO LOVE
(from "Anything Goes")

Words and Music by
COLE PORTER

16
F7(♭9) F9 Dm D♭dim7 Cm Fm
sit down to eggs and ba - con with. We'd be so
21
Cm F7 B♭/D D♭dim B♭/D E♭6
grand at the game, so care - free to - geth - er that it
freely
25
B♭6 G7 Fsus/C E♭m6/C B♭/D E♭7(♯11)
does seem a shame, that you can't see your fu - ture with
freely
30
D7 Cm9 F13(♭9) B♭ G♭7 F7 B♭(add9)
me, 'cause you'd be oh, so eas - y to love.

EVENIN' STAR

(from "110 in the Shade")

Music by
HARVEY SCHMIDT

Words by
TOM JONES

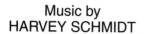

CD/TRACK 1/17

C+7(♯9)
F6/9/C
B♭maj7
mp
you search for some - thin' that is
f
Gm9
C7(♯9)
C9
F(add9)
G(add9)/C
F(add9)
lost out in the night. I
3
mp
C+7(♯9)
F6/9/C
C+7(♯9)
poco rit.
B♭maj7
reck - on you're a lot like me. I reck - on you're a lot like me. Eve - nin'
poco rit.
Gm11
a tempo
C13(♯9 ♯11)
rit.
f
Fmaj13
mp
molto rit.
star, I know.
8va
a tempo
rit.
mp
molto rit.
(with pedal)

EVERYBODY SAYS DON'T
(from "Anyone Can Whistle")

Music and Lyrics by
STEPHEN SONDHEIM

CD/TRACK 1/18

8
grass. Don't dis-turb the peace. Don't skate on the ice.
11
Well, I say do!
f
14
I say walk on the grass, it was meant to feel! I say
17
sail! Tilt at a wind-mill and if you fail, you fail!
mp

20
Ev - 'ry - bod - y says don't, Ev - 'ry - bod - y says don't. Ev - 'ry - bod - y says don't get out of
sfz
22
line. When they say that, then La - dy, that's a sign:
25
Nine times out of ten, La-dy, you are do - ing just
28
fine!

This page has been intentionally left blank in order to avoid an awkward page turn.

FIT AS A FIDDLE (AND READY FOR LOVE)

(from "Singin' in the Rain")

Words by
ARTHUR FREED

Music by
AL HOFFMAN
and AL GOODHEART

CD/TRACK 1/19

11
Eb9
Ab6
F9
church bells will be ring - ing and I'll march with Ma and Pa. How those
15
Bb7
Fm7 Bb7
church bells will be ring - ing with a hey, non-ny, non-ny, and a hot-cha - cha!
19
Fm7 Bb7 Fm7 Bb7 Eb6 Bb6 Eb6 Bb6
Hi did-dle did-dle; my ba-by's o - kay. Ask me a rid - dle; oh, what did she say?
23
Fm7 Bb7 Bb9 Eb Ab Eb Ab7 Eb
Fit as a fid - dle and ready - y for love.
8va

GROW FOR ME

(from "Little Shop of Horrors")

Words by
HOWARD ASHMAN

Music by
ALAN MENKEN

CD/TRACK 1/20

Optional start
Edim7 Fm
south - ern ex - po - sure to get you to thrive. I've pinched you back
F♯dim7 E♭/G E♭7
hard like I'm s'posed ta. You're bare - ly a - live. I've tried you at
A♭ A dim7 E♭/B♭ B dim7 Cm Cm/B♭
lev - els of mois - ture from des - ert to mud. I've
Spoken: Well, I guess a few drops couldn't hurt.
F7 E♭/G Fm7(♭5)/A♭ F7/A B♭7 B♭7/D
cresc.
giv - en you grow-lights and min - er - al sup - ple - ments. What do you want from me? Blood?
cresc.

HAIR

(from "Hair")

Lyrics by
JAMES RADO and GEROME RAGNI

Music by
GALT MacDERMOT

CD/TRACK 1/21

Moderate rock (♩ = 120)

9
Gm
B♭
Cm7
A♭
Cm
E♭
ev - ’ry-where, dad-dy, dad-dy. Hair.
Flow it,
12
B♭/F
E♭7/G
A♭
B♭
Cm
show it, long as God can grow it my hair.
15

HEART
(from "Damn Yankees")

Words and Music by
RICHARD ADLER and JERRY ROSS

CD/TRACK 1/22

C7 F F/E♭ D7 Gm7
miles 'n' miles 'n' miles of heart. Oh, it's fine to be a gen-ius of course, but
Gm7(♭5) A dim7 E♭dim7 D7
keep that old horse be-fore the cart, So what the
B♭6 B dim7 Dm7/C Cm6/E♭ D9
heck's the use of cry-in'? Why should we curse? We've got-ta get bet-ter 'cause we can't get worse! And to
Gm7 B♭/C C7 F C7 F
add to it, We've got heart!

HER FACE

(from "Carnival")

Words and Music by
BOB MERRILL

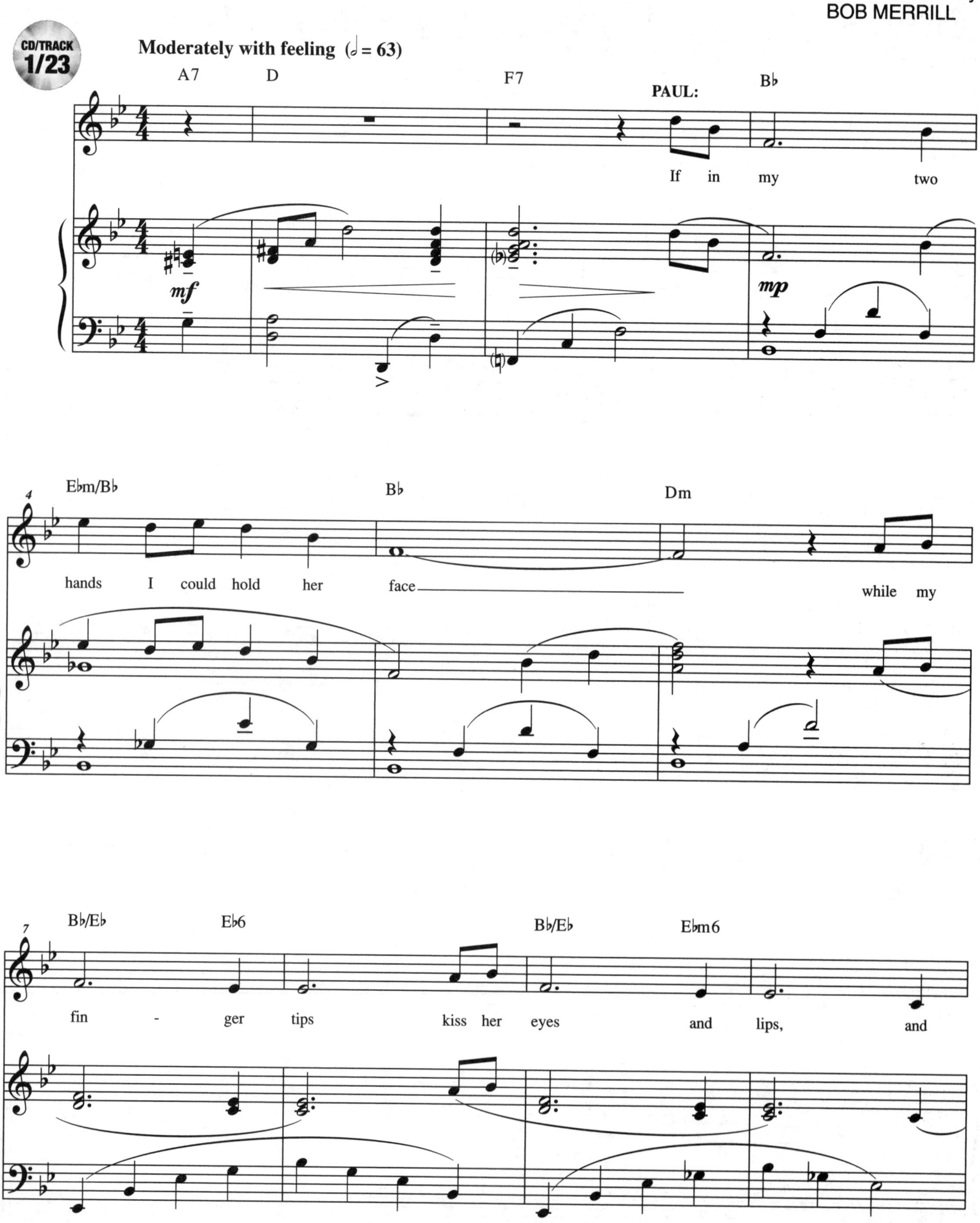

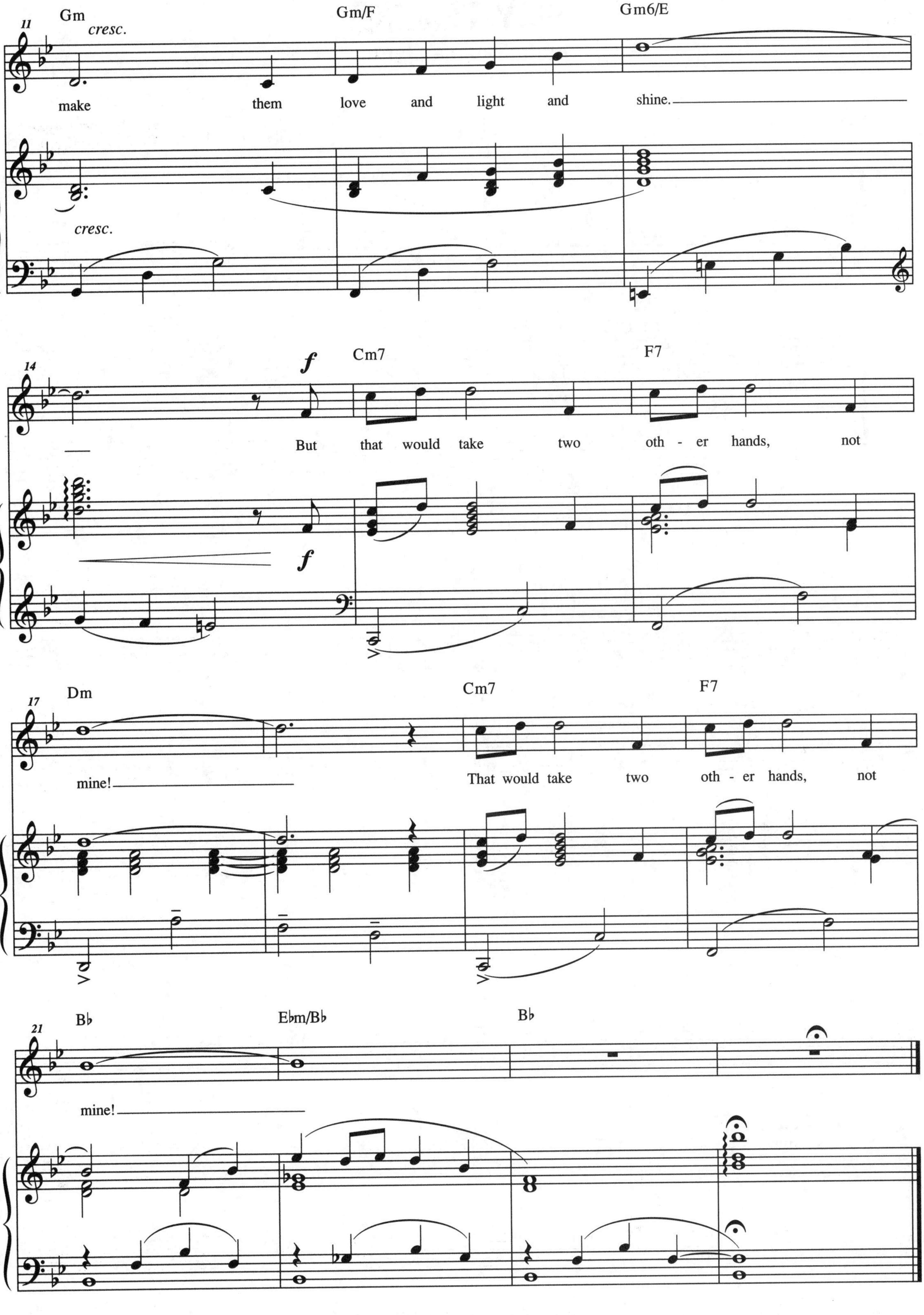
11
Gm
cresc.
Gm/F
Gm6/E
make them love and light and shine.
cresc.
14
f
Cm7
F7
But that would take two oth - er hands, not
f
17
Dm
Cm7
F7
mine!
That would take two oth - er hands, not
21
B♭
E♭m/B♭
B♭
mine!

HEY THERE
(from "Pajama Game")

Words and Music by
RICHARD ADLER and JERRY ROSS

CD/TRACK 1/24

Slow and expressively (♩ = 90)

12
F/C E+7/C Cm/E♭ D+7 D7 Gm7
broth - er? Or are you not see - ing things too
15
Gm7(♭5) F E♭6 D7
clear, Are you just too far gone to hear, Is it
18
Gm7 C7 C9 Fmaj7/C C7
all go - ing in one ear and out the
21
E/F F Gm7 C7 C7(♭9) F
oth - er?

HIGHWAY MILES
(from "The Flood")

Words and Music by
PETER MILLS

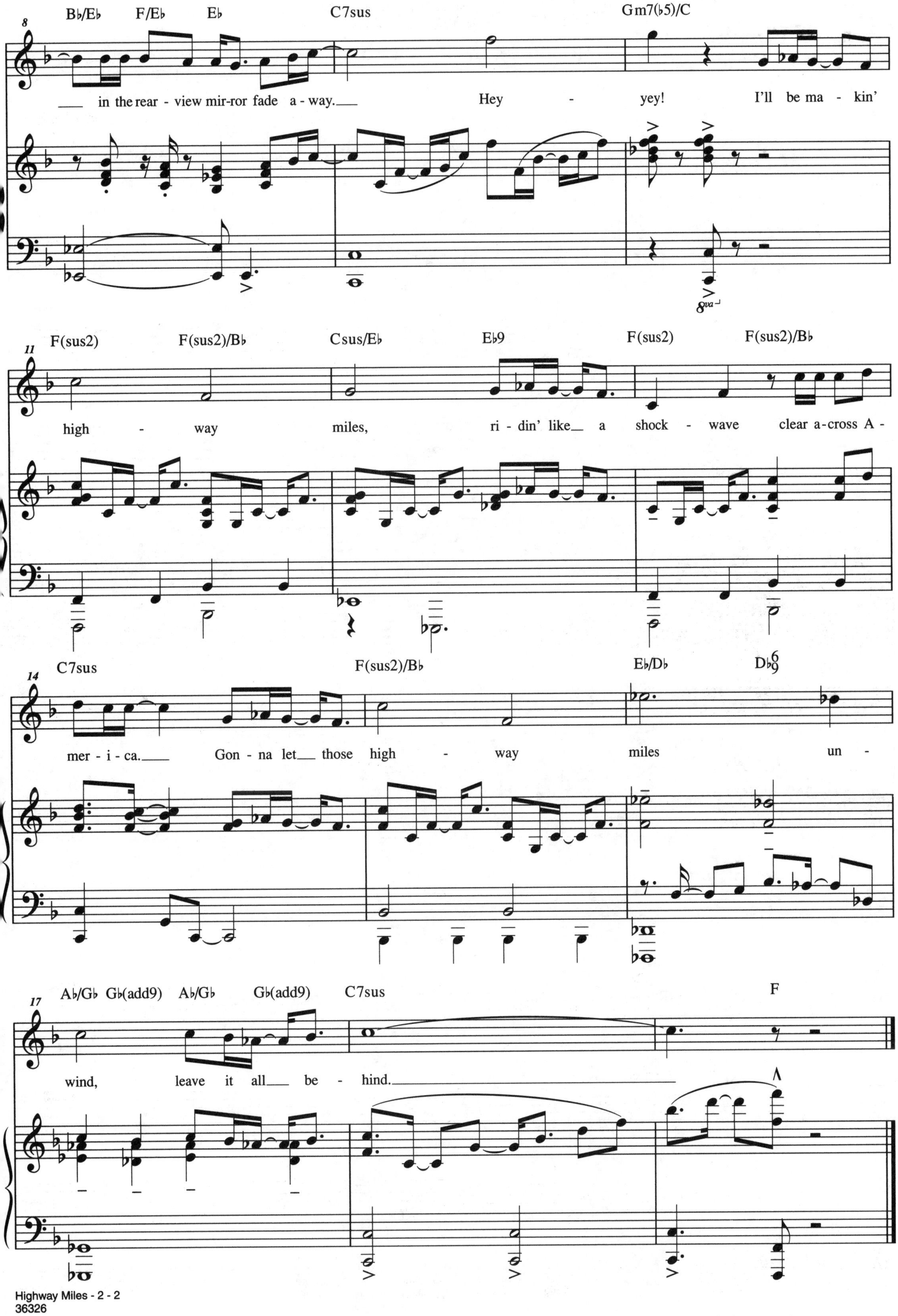
B♭/E♭ F/E♭ E♭ C7sus Gm7(♭5)/C
in the rear - view mir-ror fade a - way. Hey - yey! I'll be ma - kin'
F(sus2) F(sus2)/B♭ Csus/E♭ E♭9 F(sus2) F(sus2)/B♭
high - way miles, ri - din' like a shock - wave clear a-cross A -
C7sus F(sus2)/B♭ E♭/D♭ D♭6/9
mer - i - ca. Gon - na let those high - way miles un -
A♭/G♭ G♭(add9) A♭/G♭ G♭(add9) C7sus F
wind, leave it all be - hind.

HOME

(recorded by Michael Bublé)

Words and Music by
MICHAEL BUBLÉ, ALAN CHANG
and AMY FOSTER

10
Cmaj9
Em9
send them, but I know that it's just not e-nough.
My words were cold
12
Fmaj9
Dsus
and flat, and you de-serve more than
14
D
G
G/F♯
that.
An-oth-er win-ter day has come and gone a-way
16
Em7
D
Cmaj7
Dsus
G
rit.
3
in ei-ther Par-is or Rome, and I wan-na go home.
I've got to go home.
rit.

HOW LUCKY YOU ARE

(from "Seussical the Musical")

Lyrics by
LYNN AHRENS

Music by
STEPHEN FLAHERTY

CD/TRACK 1/27

F Fmaj7 Fdim7
hap - py you're here. Think of life as a thrill! And if
F Am/E Cm/E♭ D7
worse comes to worse (as we all know it will),
mp
Dm7/G G7 C7sus/G C9 F F7/E♭
tell your - self how luck - y you are! How luck - y, how luck -
mf
B♭/D B♭m6/D♭ F/C F+/C♯ Dm D♭+ C7 F
- y, how luck - y, how luck - y, how luck - y, how luck - y you are!

HUSHABYE MOUNTAIN

(from "Chitty Chitty Bang Bang")

CD/TRACK 1/28

Words and Music by
RICHARD M. SHERMAN
& ROBERT B. SHERMAN

Moderate waltz (♩ = 120)

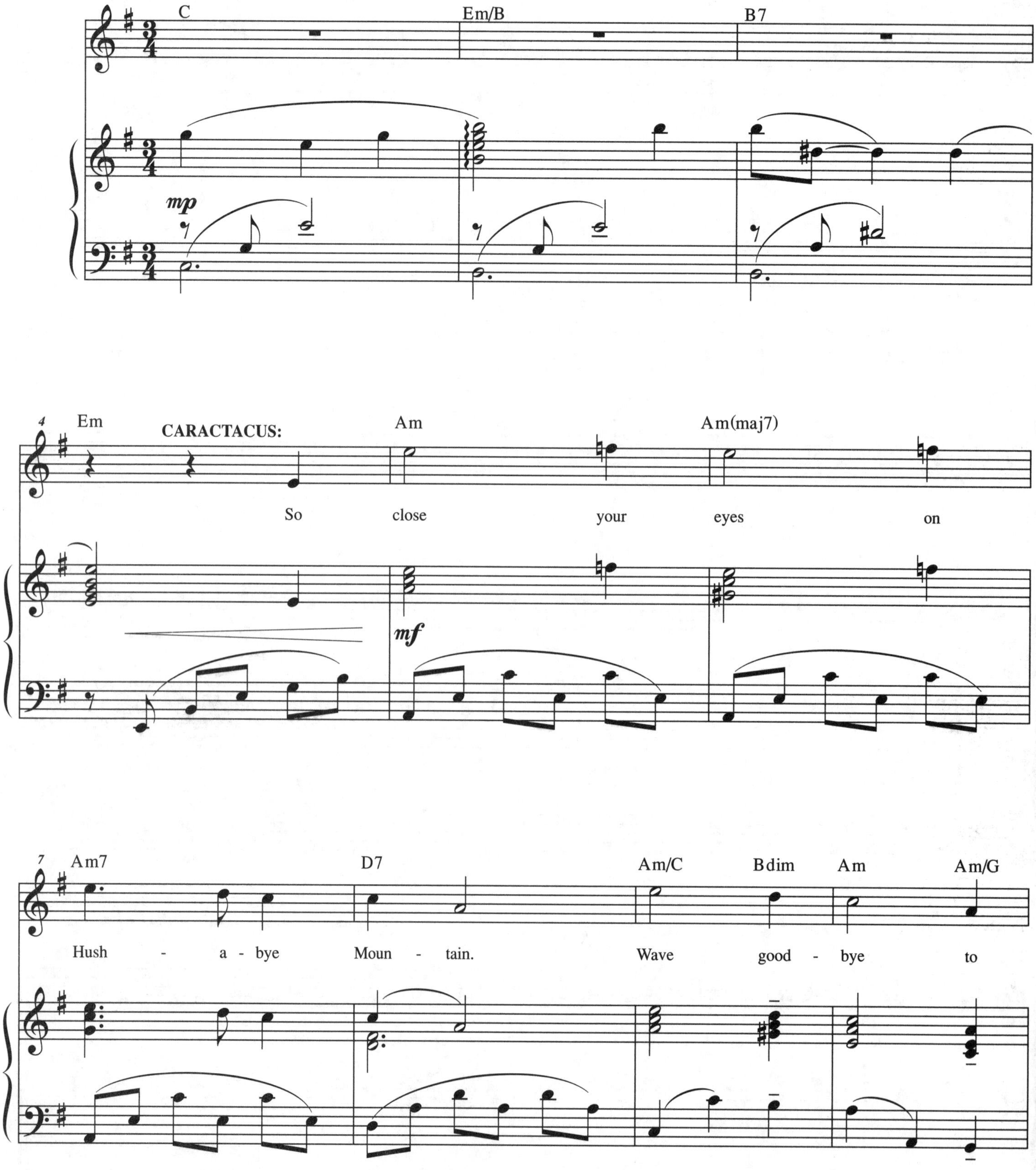

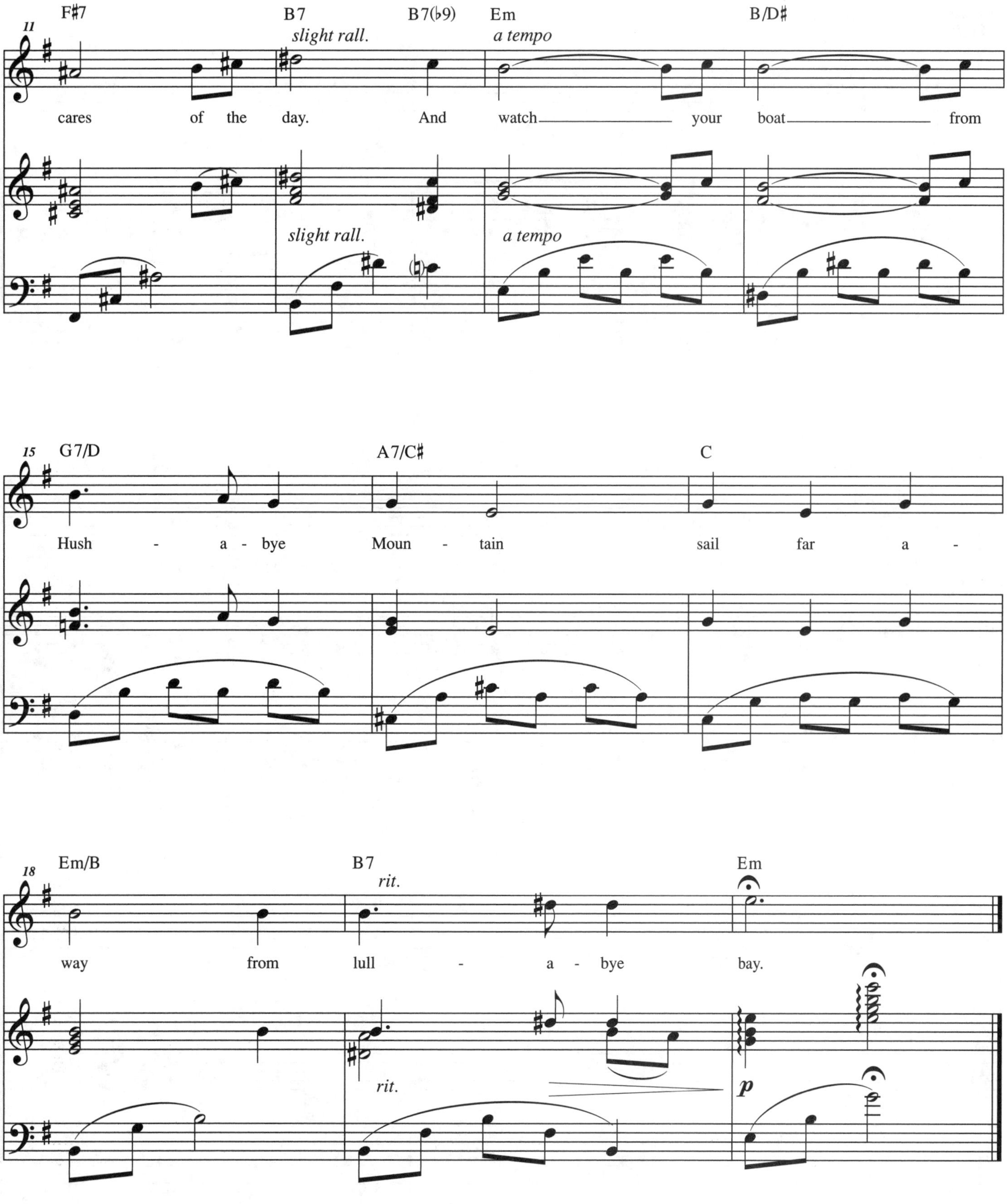
11
F♯7
B7
B7(♭9)
Em
B/D♯
slight rall.
a tempo
cares of the day. And watch your boat from
slight rall.
a tempo
15
G7/D
A7/C♯
C
Hush - a - bye Moun - tain sail far a -
18
Em/B
B7
Em
rit.
way from lull - a - bye bay.
rit.
p

I CAN SEE IT
(from "The Fantasticks")

Lyrics by
HARVEY SCHMIDT

Music by
TOM JONES

CD/TRACK 1/29

Brightly (♩ = 188)

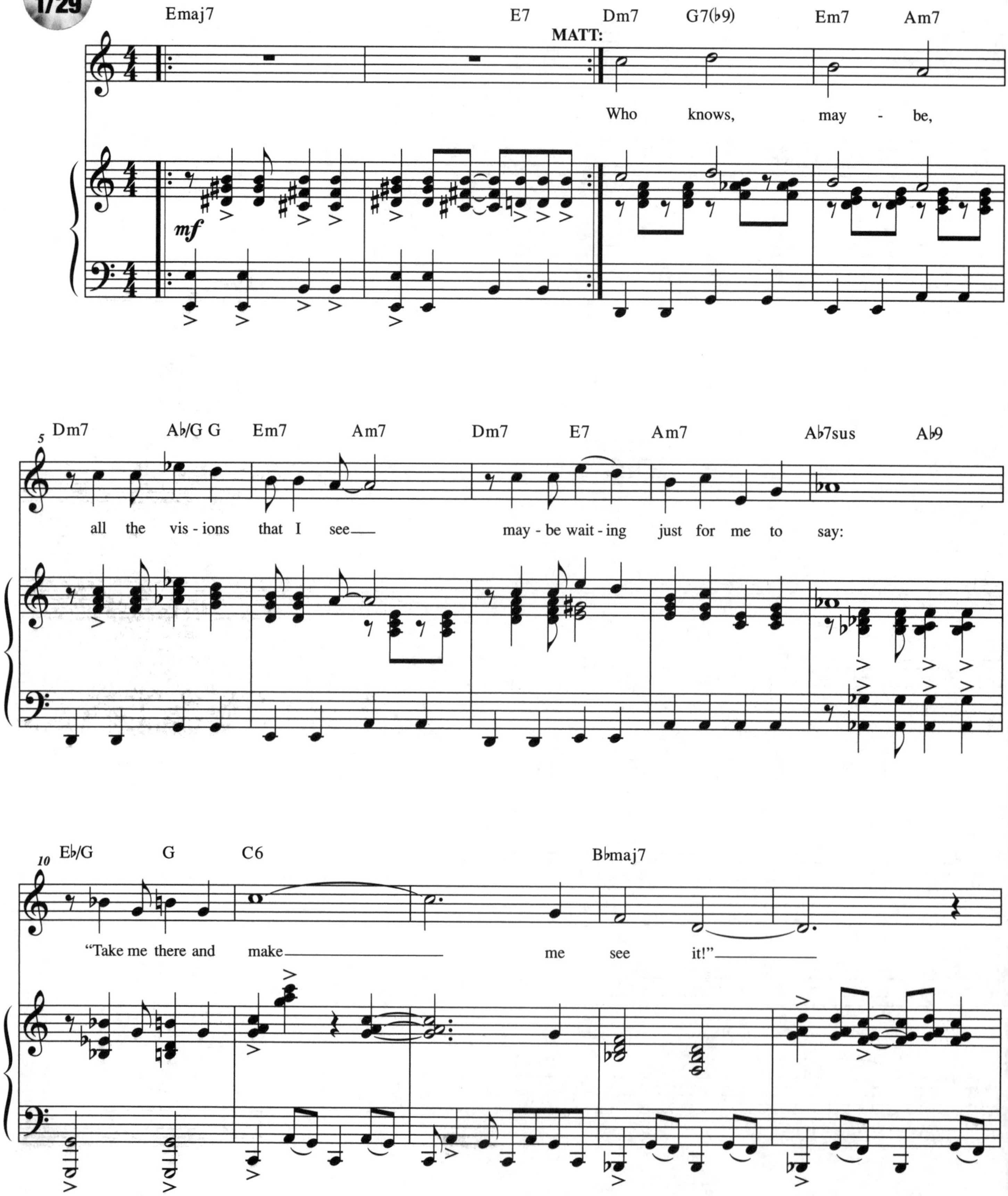

I Can See It - 2 - 1
36326

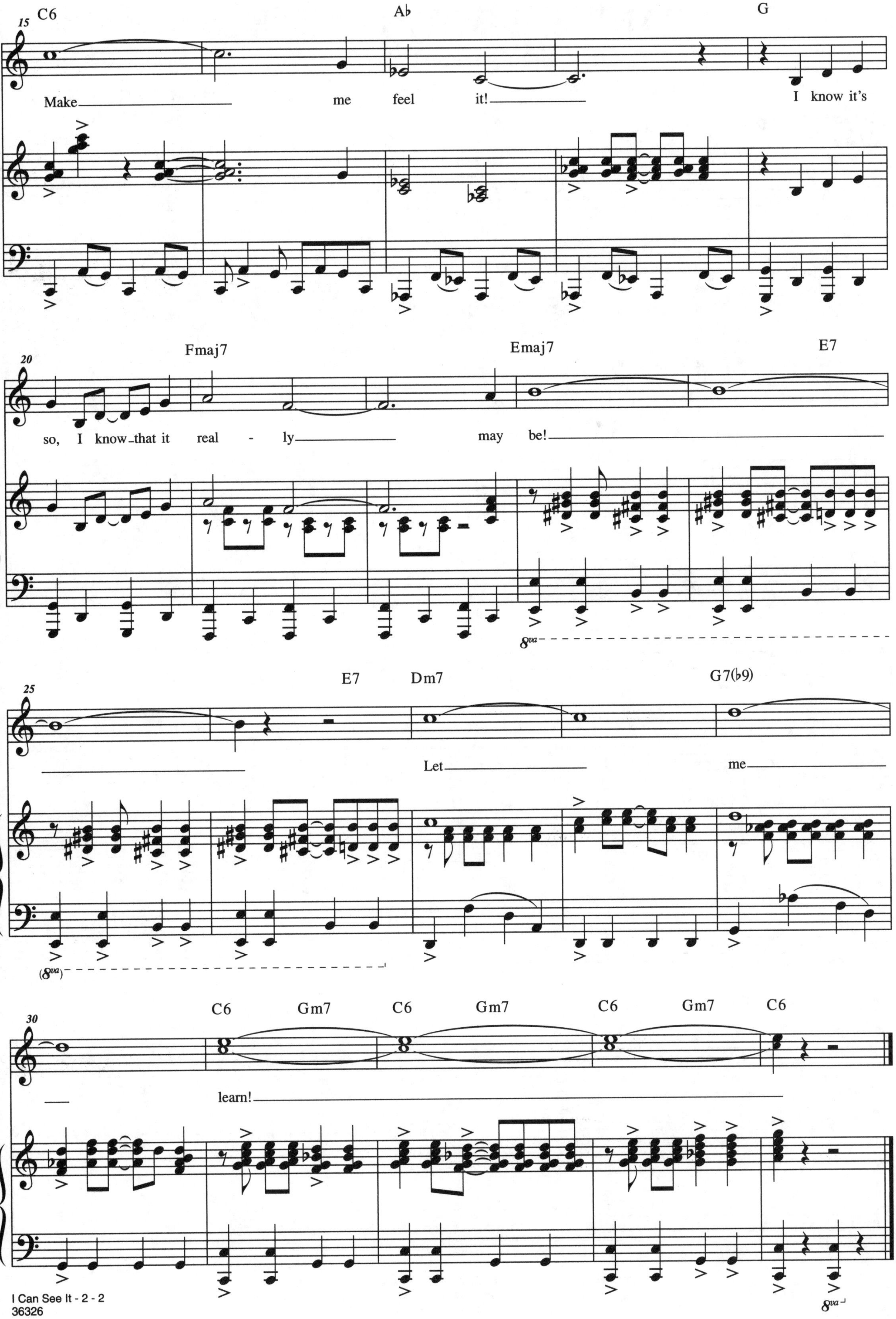
C6
A♭
G
Make me feel it!
I know it's
Fmaj7
Emaj7
E7
so, I know that it real - ly may be!
8va
E7
Dm7
G7(♭9)
Let me
(8va)
C6
Gm7
C6
Gm7
C6
Gm7
C6
learn!
8va

I CAN'T BE BOTHERED NOW

(from "Crazy for You")

Music and Lyrics by GEORGE GERSHWIN
and IRA GERSHWIN

CD/TRACK 1/30

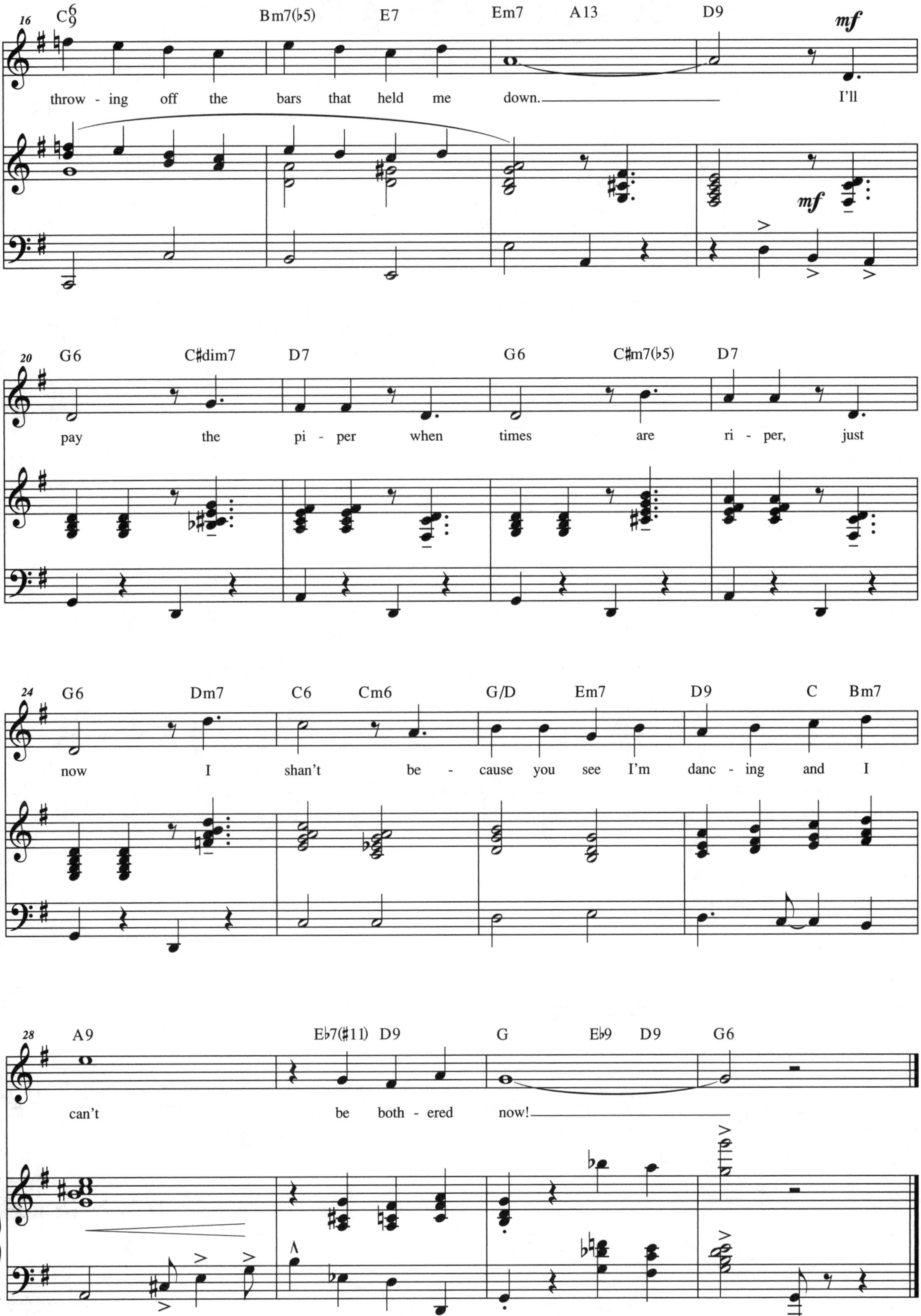
16
C6/9 Bm7(♭5) E7 Em7 A13 D9
mf
throw - ing off the bars that held me down. I'll
20
G6 C♯dim7 D7 G6 C♯m7(♭5) D7
pay the pi - per when times are ri - per, just
24
G6 Dm7 C6 Cm6 G/D Em7 D9 C Bm7
now I shan't be - cause you see I'm danc - ing and I
28
A9 E♭7(♯11) D9 G E♭9 D9 G6
can't be both - ered now!

I COULD WRITE A BOOK

(from "Pal Joey")

Words by
LORENZ HART

Music by
RICHARD RODGERS

CD/TRACK 1/31

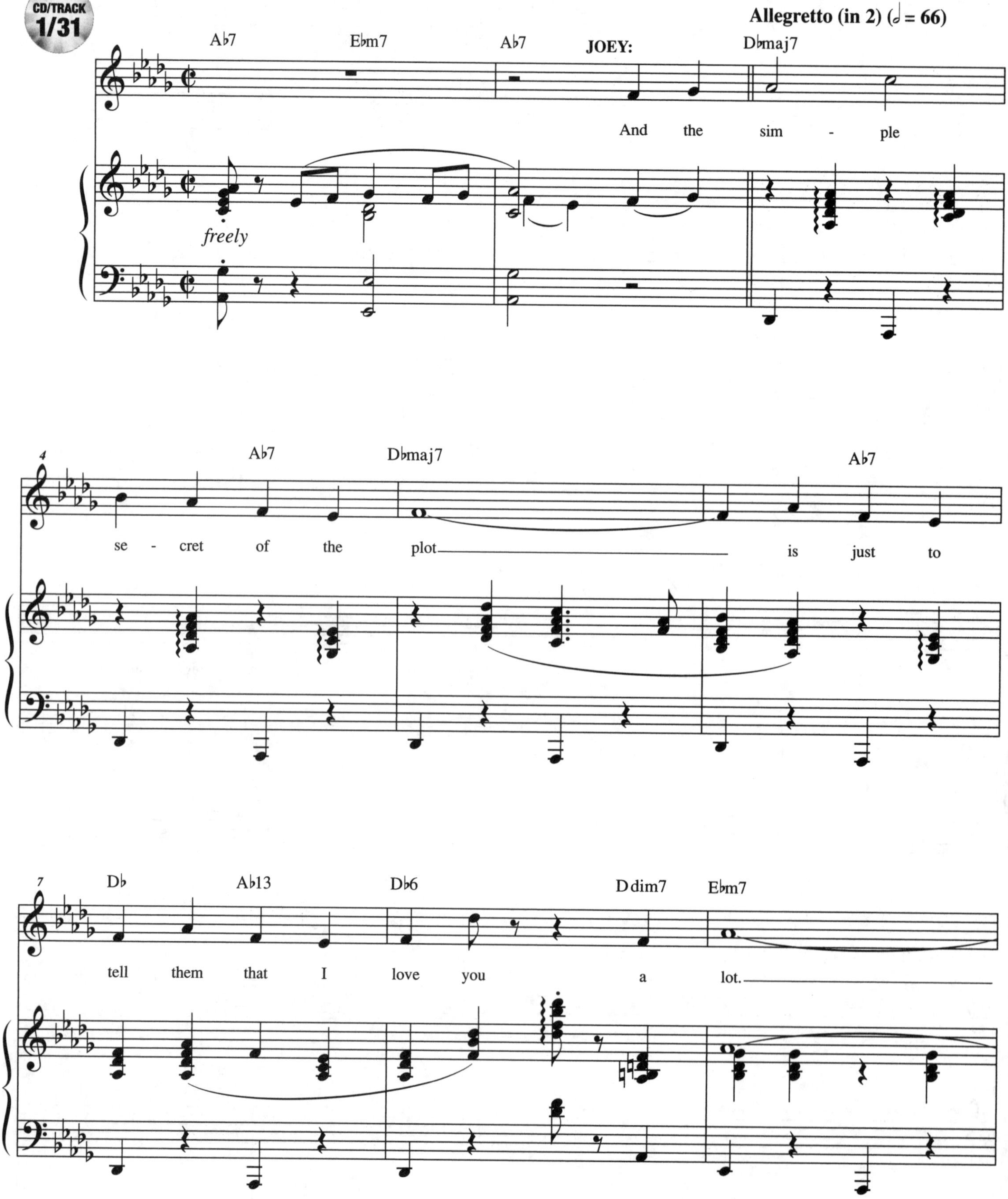

10
A♭7
Db/F
Edim7
E♭m7
A♭9
— Then the world dis - cov - ers, as
13
A♭m7
D♭7
G♭maj7
E♭m7
D♭/A♭
F+
my book ends, how to make two
16
G♭6
E♭m7
A♭7
D♭
lov - ers of friends.

I LOVE TO RHYME

(from "Goldwyn Follies" 1938)

CD/TRACK 1/32

Music and Lyrics by
GEORGE GERSHWIN and IRA GERSHWIN

Moderato, with spirit (𝅗𝅥 = 92)

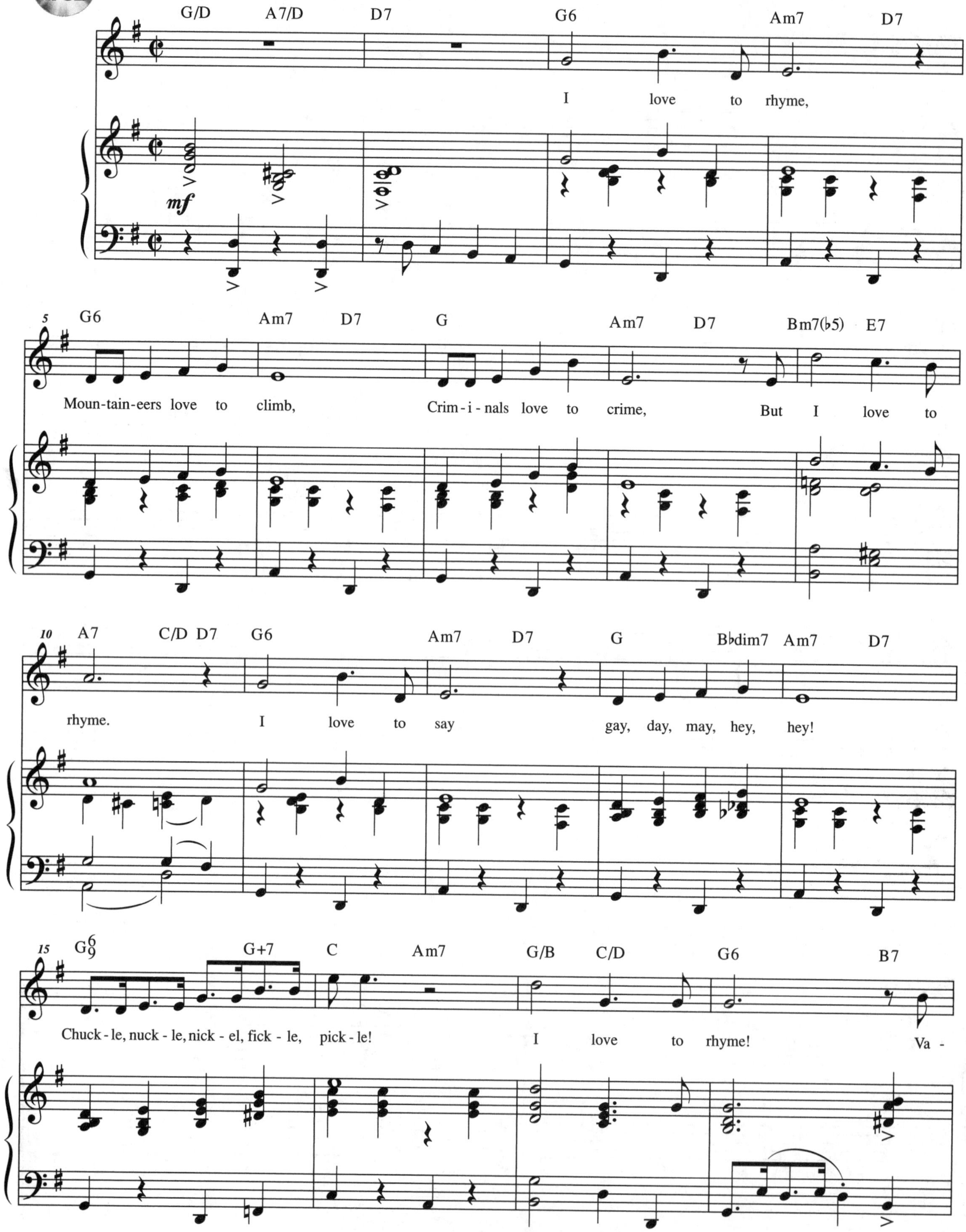

19
Em Em/G Am C/A♯ Em/B F♯+7 B+7 B7
ri - e - ty, so - ci - e - ty, pro - pri - e - ty, There's no stop - ping when you've be - gun; Ca -
23
Em Em/G Am Cm G/D A9/D C6/D D7
pa - ci - ty, ve - ra - ci - ty, au - da - ci - ty, Did you ev - er know such fun?
27
G6 Am7 D7 Gmaj7 Am7 D7
I love to rhyme, and would - n't it be sub - lime if
31
G Em7 A7 Cmaj9/D G6/9
one day it could be that you rhyme with me?
8va

I MARRIED AN ANGEL

(from "I Married an Angel")

Words by
LORENZ HART

Music by
RICHARD RODGERS

CD/TRACK 1/33

Moderate ballad (𝅗𝅥 = 63)

11
F
a tempo
C7/G
F/A
Dm
Gm7
C7
F/A
Dm
Now you've heard, I mar-ried an an - gel.
a tempo
15
Gm7
C7
F
D7
Gm7
C7
F
This beau - ti - ful change - 'll be aw - f'lly good for me.

I MET A GIRL

(from "Bells are Ringing")

Words by
BETTY COMDEN and ADOLPH GREEN

Music by
JULE STYNE

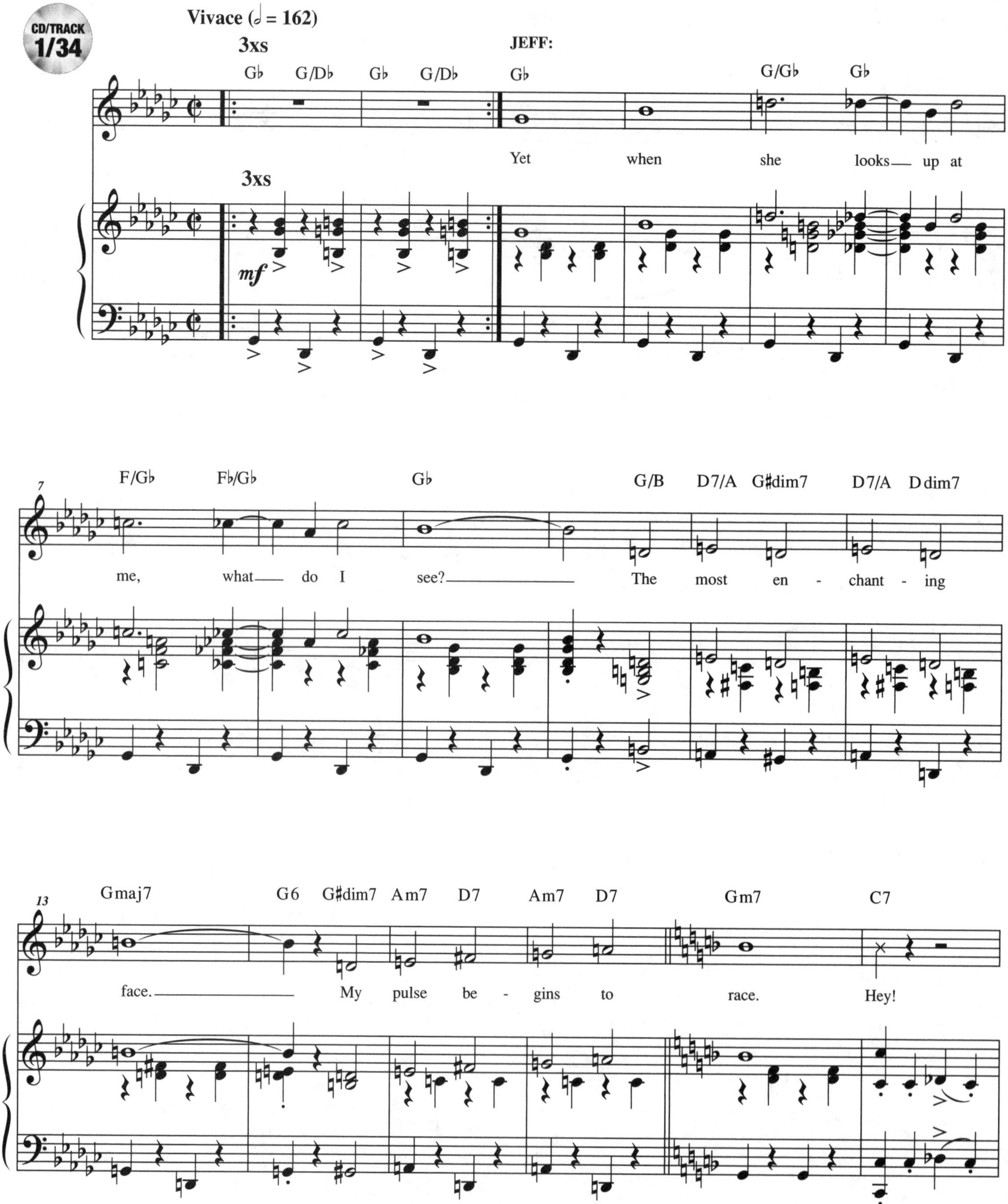

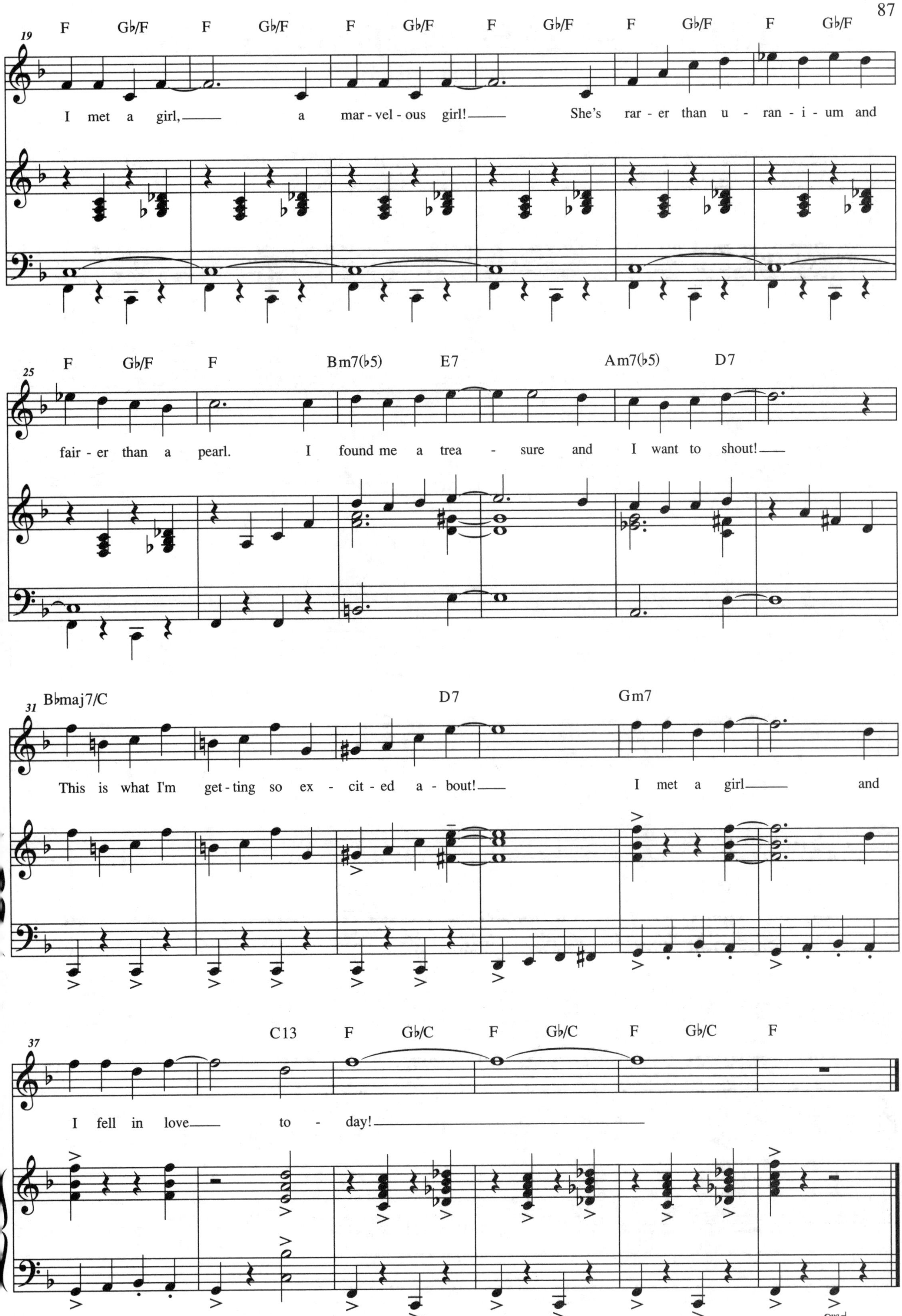
19
F Gb/F F Gb/F F Gb/F F Gb/F F Gb/F F Gb/F
I met a girl, a mar-vel-ous girl! She's rar-er than u-ran-i-um and
25
F Gb/F F Bm7(b5) E7 Am7(b5) D7
fair-er than a pearl. I found me a trea-sure and I want to shout!
31
Bbmaj7/C D7 Gm7
This is what I'm get-ting so ex-cit-ed a-bout! I met a girl and
37
C13 F Gb/C F Gb/C F Gb/C F
I fell in love to-day!
8va

I WANT TO BE SEEN WITH YOU TONIGHT

(from "Funny Girl")

Words by
BOB MERRILL

Music by
JULE STYNE

CD/TRACK 1/35

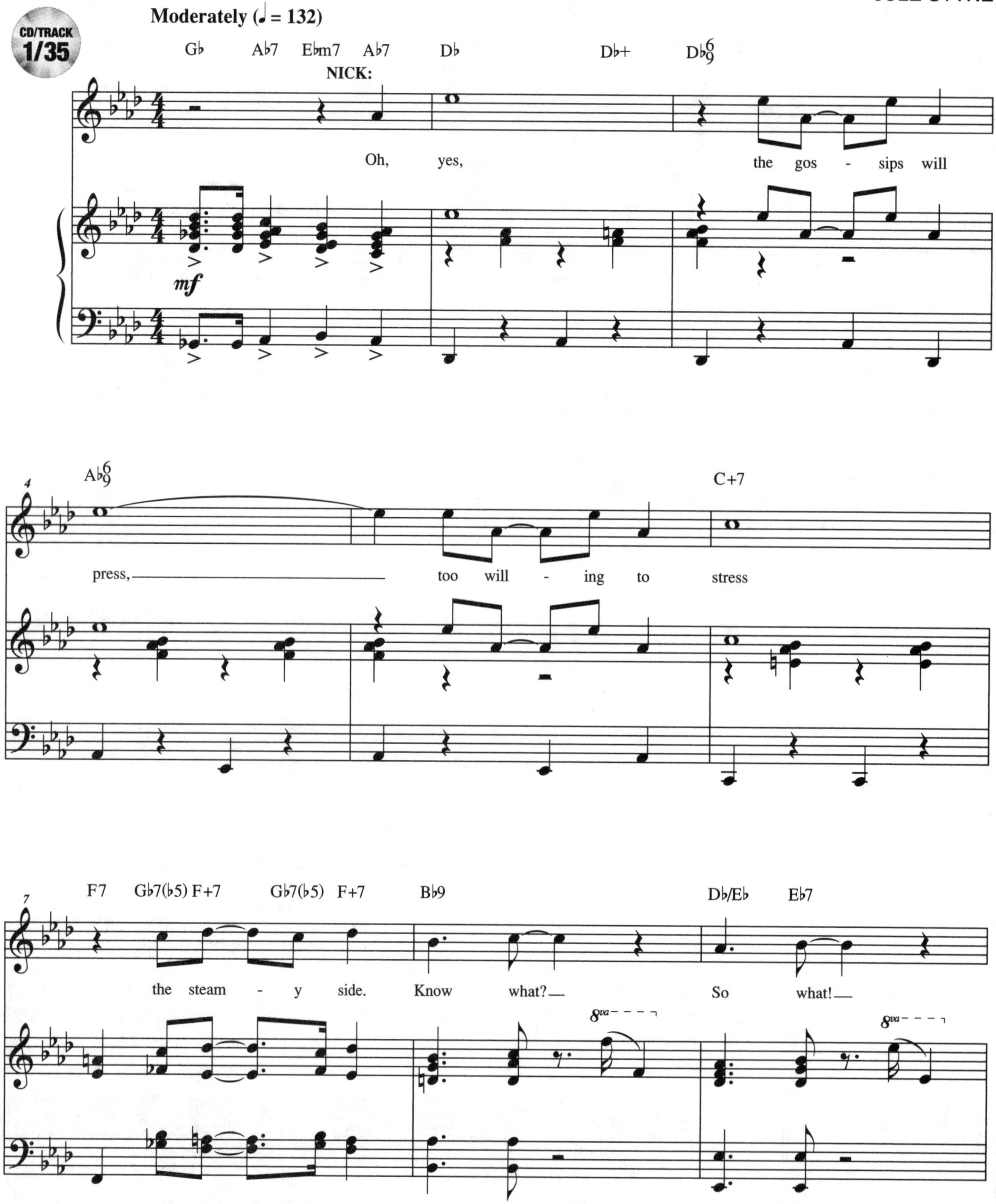

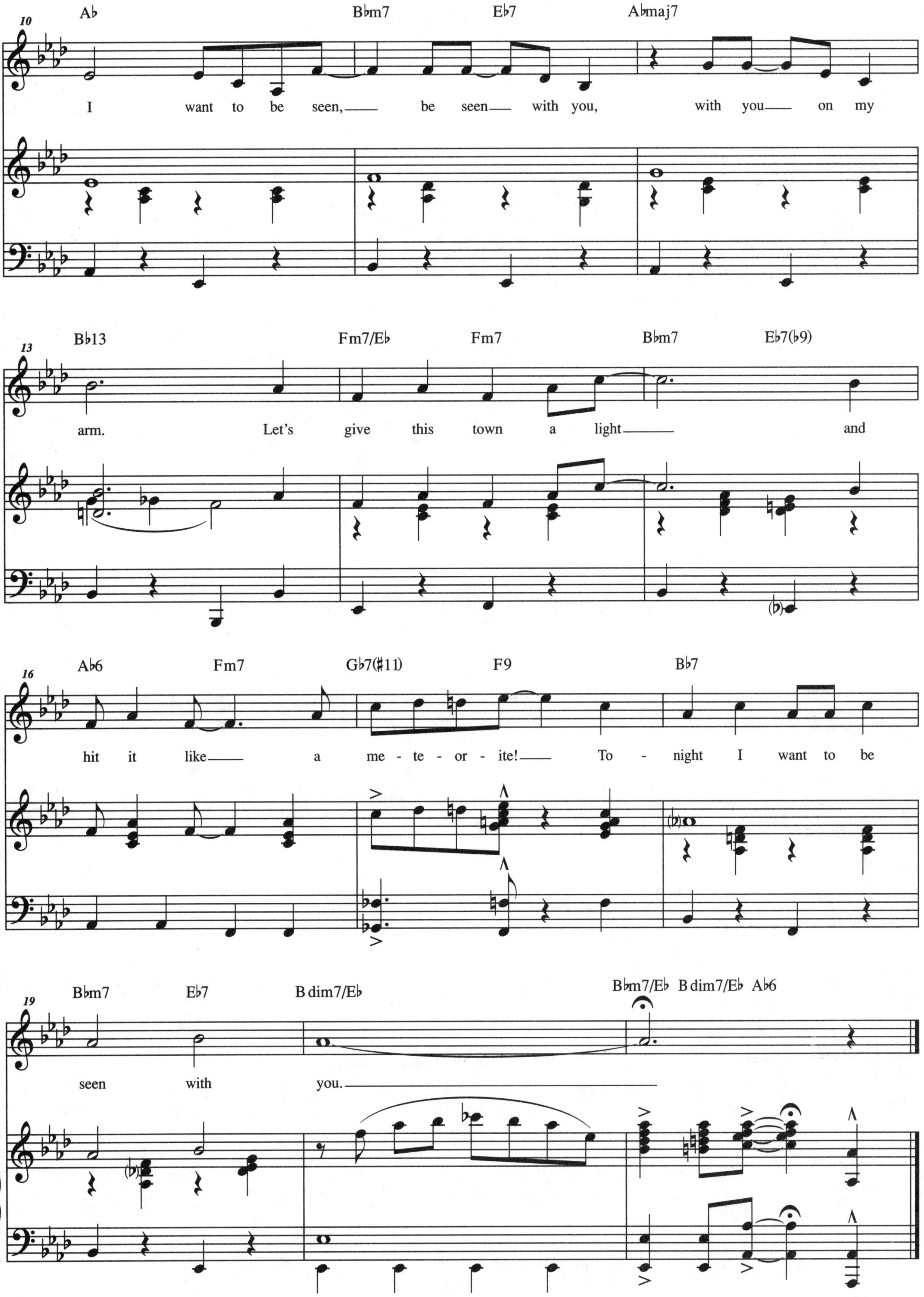
10
A♭
B♭m7
E♭7
A♭maj7
I want to be seen, be seen with you, with you on my
13
B♭13
Fm7/E♭
Fm7
B♭m7
E♭7(♭9)
arm. Let's give this town a light and
16
A♭6
Fm7
G♭7(♯11)
F9
B♭7
hit it like a me - te - or - ite! To - night I want to be
19
B♭m7
E♭7
B dim7/E♭
B♭m7/E♭
B dim7/E♭
A♭6
seen with you.

I WANT TO MAKE MAGIC

(from "Fame: The Musical")

Lyrics by
JACQUES LEVY

Music by
STEVE MARGOSHES

CD/TRACK
1/36

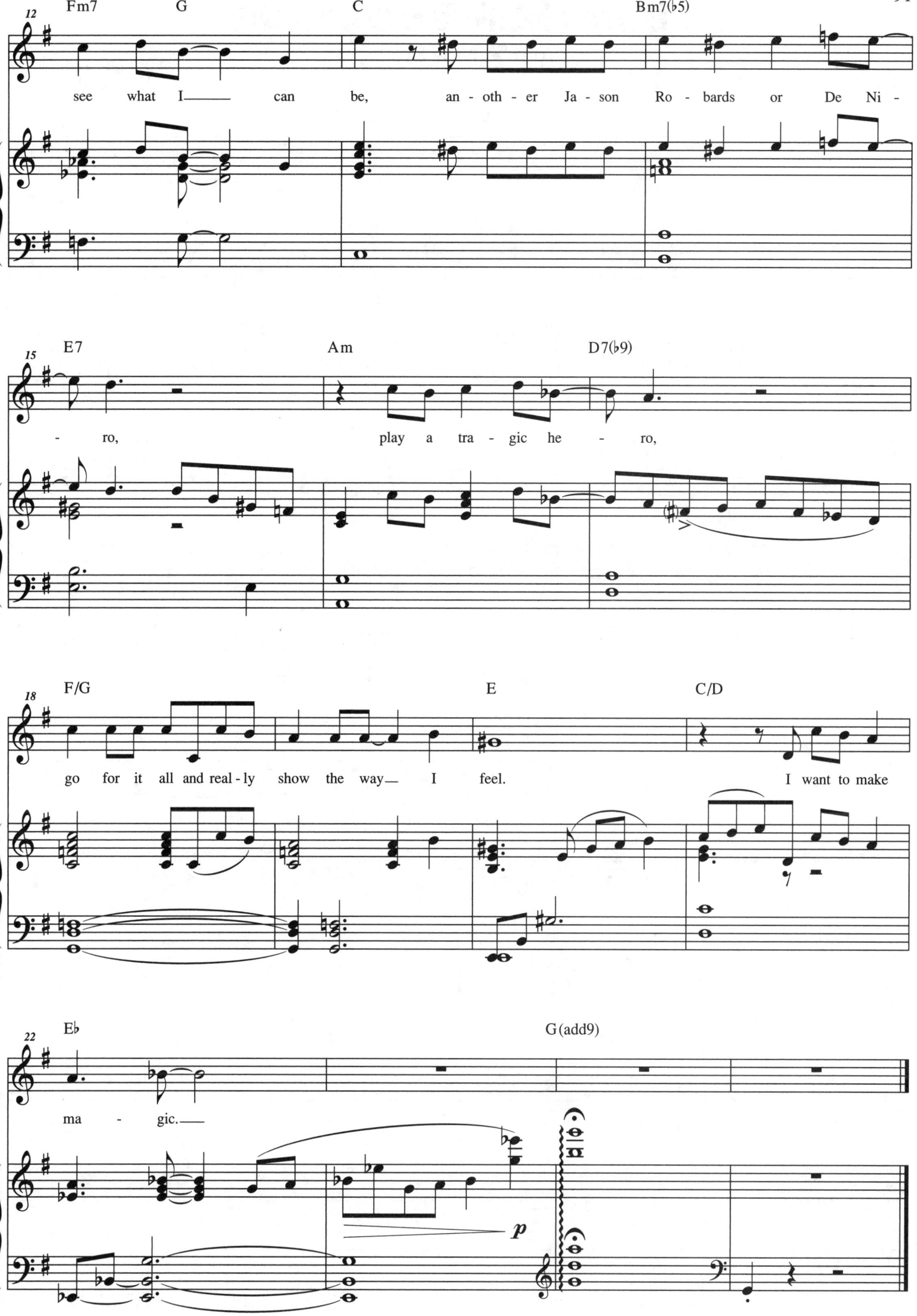
12
Fm7 G C Bm7(♭5)
see what I___ can be, an - oth - er Ja - son Ro - bards or De Ni -
15
E7 Am D7(♭9)
- ro, play a tra - gic he - ro,
18
F/G E C/D
go for it all and real - ly show the way___ I feel. I want to make
22
E♭ G(add9)
ma - gic.___
p

I'D RATHER BE SAILING

(from "A New Brain")

Words and Music by
WILLIAM FINN

CD/TRACK 1/37

Bb7(b9)
Bb9
Ebm7
mp
the wind is in my face, the sea is in -
Ebm7/Db
Ab7/C
Abm7(b5)/Cb
Gb(add9)
p
Bb7(b9)
cred - i - bly blue. And I'd rath-er be sail - ing, yes,
Ebm7
Gb/Db
Abm7
Abm7/Db
I'd wan-na go sail, and then come home
Db
Gb(add9)
Gb/E
B/Eb
Bm/D
Gb
to you.

I'M ALIVE
(from "Next to Normal")

Lyrics by
BRIAN YORKEY

Music by
TOM KITT

CD/TRACK 1/38

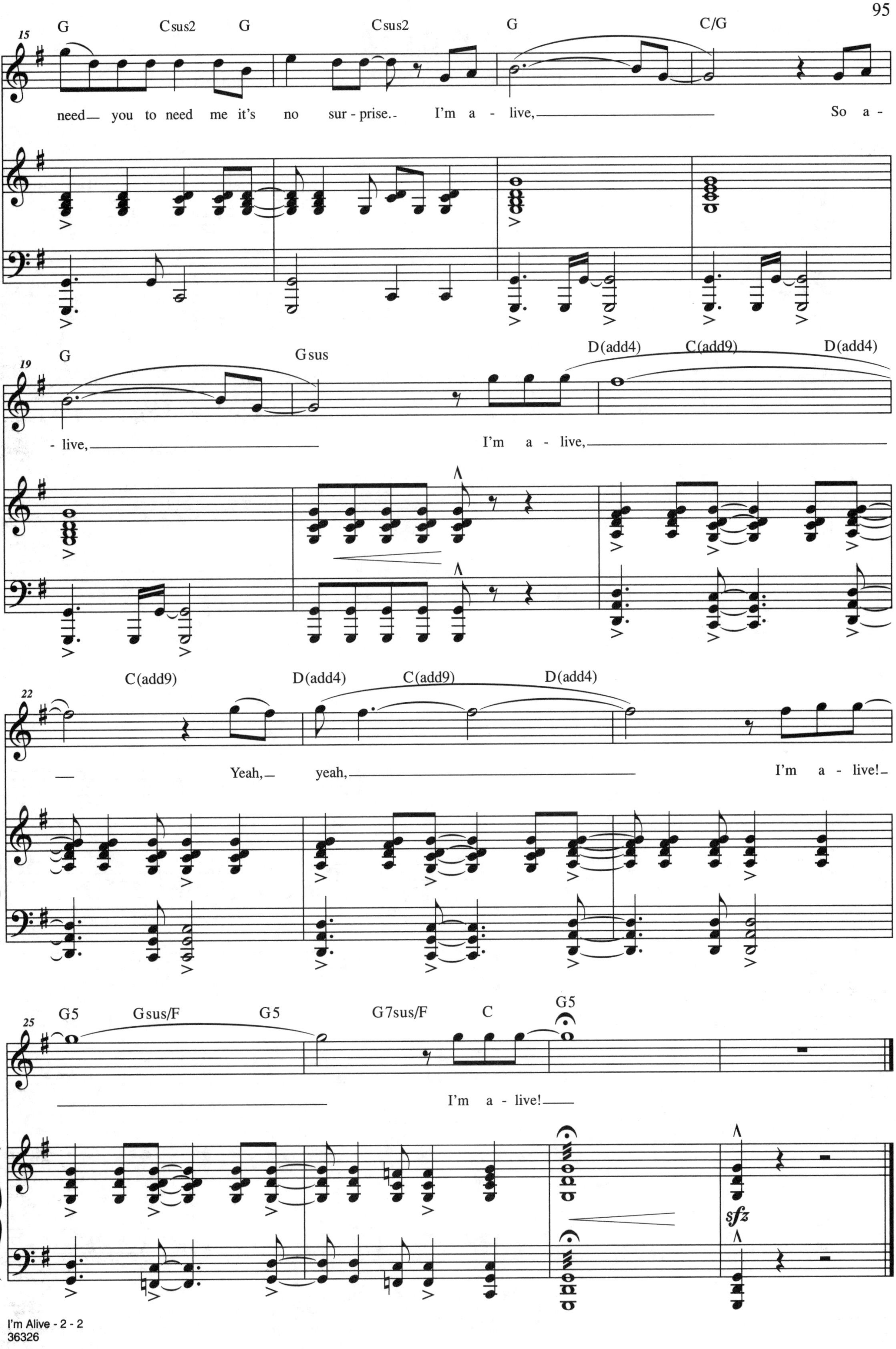
15
G Csus2 G Csus2 G C/G
need you to need me it's no sur - prise. I'm a - live, So a -
19
G Gsus D(add4) C(add9) D(add4)
- live, I'm a - live,
22
C(add9) D(add4) C(add9) D(add4)
Yeah, yeah, I'm a - live!
25
G5 Gsus/F G5 G7sus/F C G5
I'm a - live!
sfz

I'M CALM

(from "A Funny Thing Happened on the Way to the Forum")

Words and Music by
STEPHEN SONDHEIM

CD/TRACK 1/39

(relaxed tempo)
20
Look: I'm calm, I'm calm, I have - n't a qualm. I'm
(relaxed tempo)
25
ut - ter - ly un - der con - trol.
rubato
Let noth - ing con -
rubato
30
(yawn)
fuse me, or faze me... Ex - cuse me... I'm calm,
oh, so
35
calm, Oh, so...
Presto (in 1)
(running away hysterically)

I'M NOT THAT SMART

(from "The 25th Annual Putnam County Spelling Bee")

Words and Music by
WILLIAM FINN

CD/TRACK 1/40

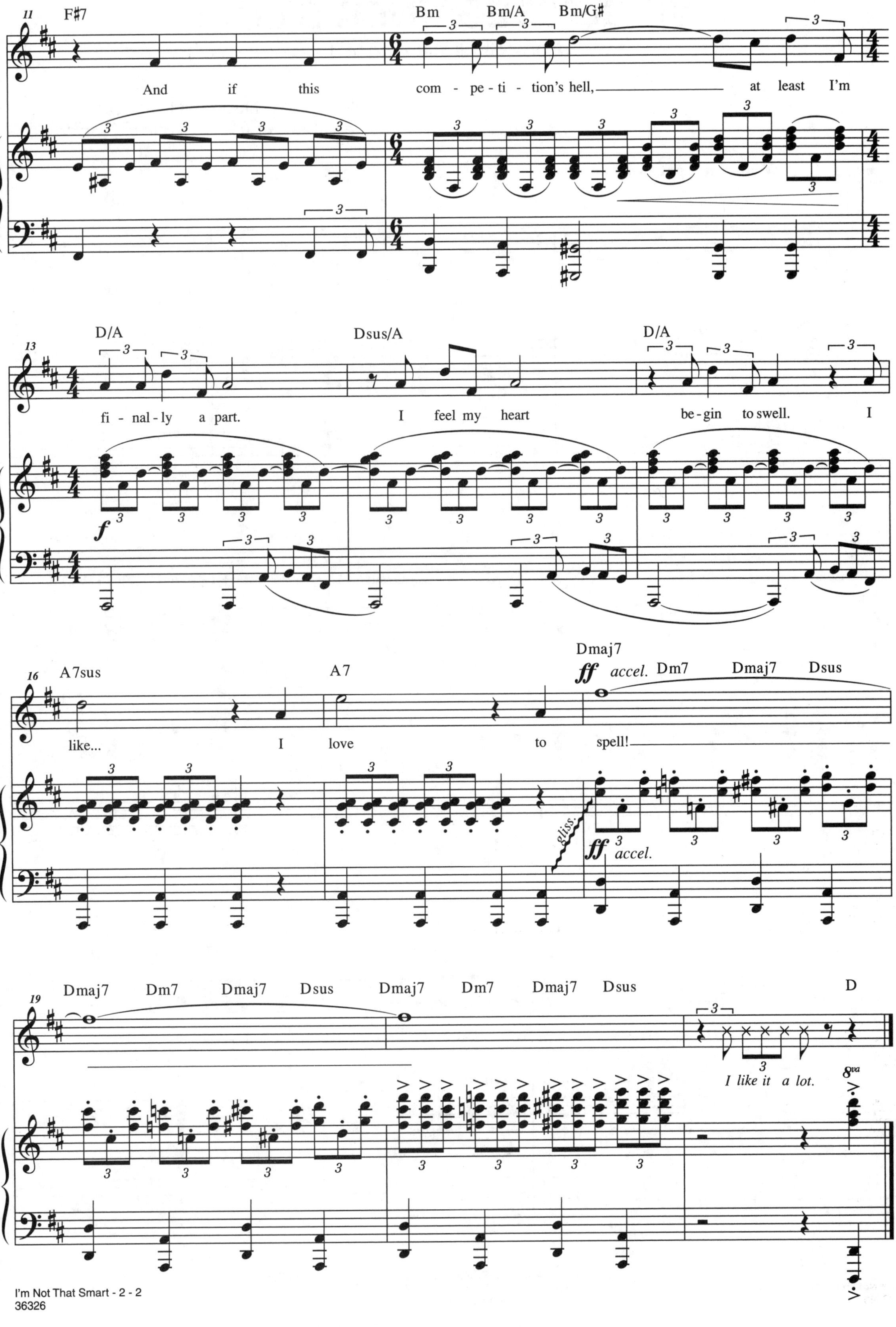
11
F♯7
Bm
Bm/A
Bm/G♯
And if this com - pe - ti - tion's hell, at least I'm
13
D/A
Dsus/A
D/A
fi - nal - ly a part. I feel my heart be - gin to swell. I
16
A7sus
A7
Dmaj7
ff accel.
Dm7
Dmaj7
Dsus
like... I love to spell!
gliss.
19
Dmaj7
Dm7
Dmaj7
Dsus
Dmaj7
Dm7
Dmaj7
Dsus
D
I like it a lot.
8va

I'VE GOT BEGINNER'S LUCK

(from "Shall We Dance")

Music and Lyrics by
GEORGE GERSHWIN and IRA GERSHWIN

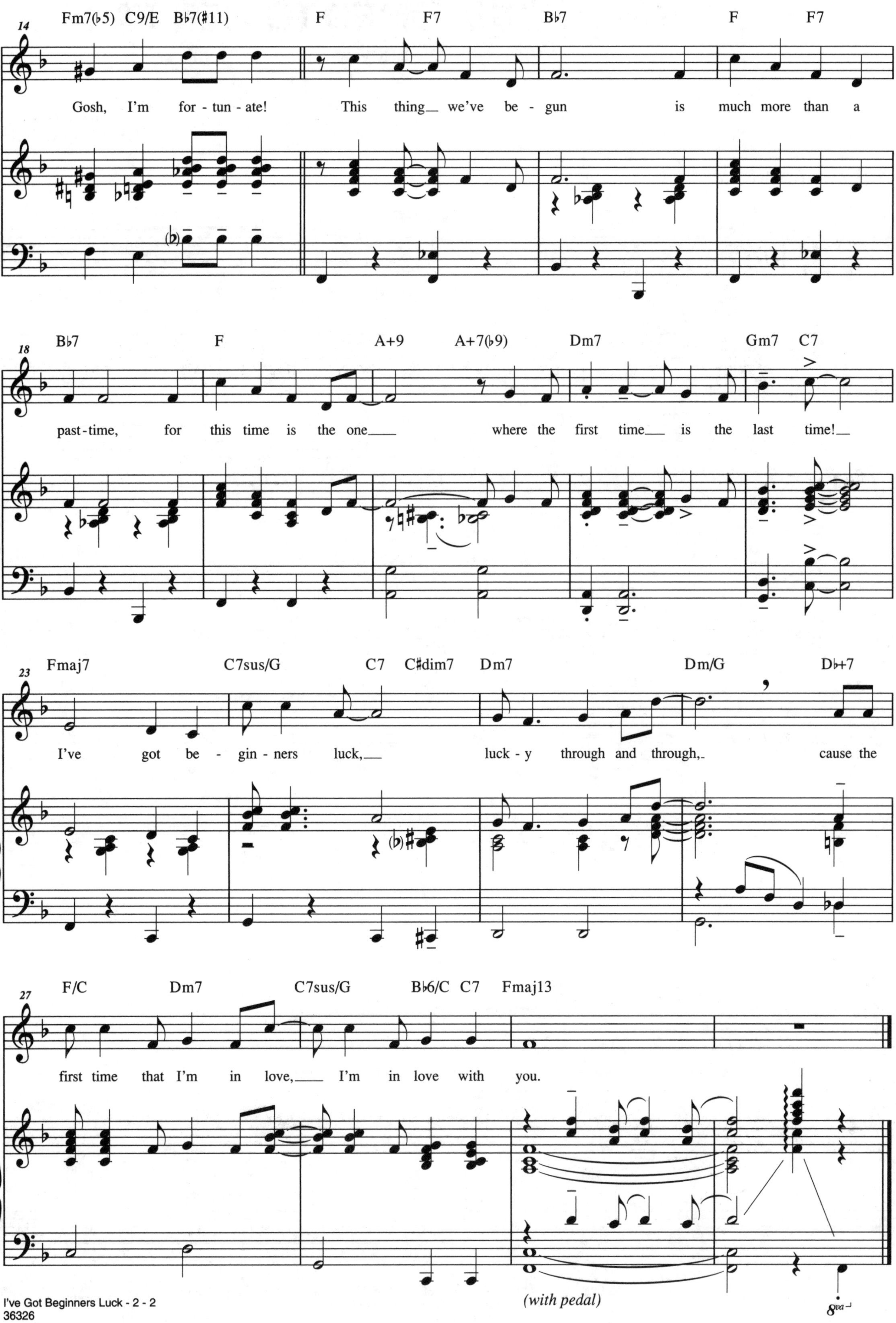
Optional start
14
Fm7(♭5) C9/E B♭7(♯11) F F7 B♭7 F F7
Gosh, I'm for - tun - ate! This thing__ we've be - gun is much more than a
18
B♭7 F A+9 A+7(♭9) Dm7 Gm7 C7
past-time, for this time is the one__ where the first time__ is the last time!__
23
Fmaj7 C7sus/G C7 C♯dim7 Dm7 Dm/G D♭+7
I've got be - gin - ners luck,__ luck - y through and through,_ cause the
27
F/C Dm7 C7sus/G B♭6/C C7 Fmaj13
first time that I'm in love,__ I'm in love with you.
(with pedal)
8va

I'VE GROWN ACCUSTOMED TO HER FACE

(from "My Fair Lady")

Words by
ALAN JAY LERNER

Music by
FREDERICK LOEWE

CD/TRACK 1/42

Tenderly (♩ = 96)

10
Dm7 G9 Cmaj7
ups, her downs are sec - ond na - ture to me now, like breath - ing
13
Dm7 G7 Cmaj7 F6 B/F♯
out and breath - ing in. I was se - rene - ly in - de - pen - dent and con -
16
C/G A+7 Dm7 G7 E+7 A+7
pp
tent be - fore we met. Sure - ly I could al - ways be that way a - gain, and yet I've grown ac -
pp
19
D9 Fm C/G Em7 Dm9 F/G C
p
cus - tomed to her looks, ac - cus - tomed to her voice, ac - cus - tomed to her face.
p
8va

IF EVER I WOULD LEAVE YOU

(from "Camelot")

Words by
ALAN JAY LERNER

Music by
FREDERICK LOEWE

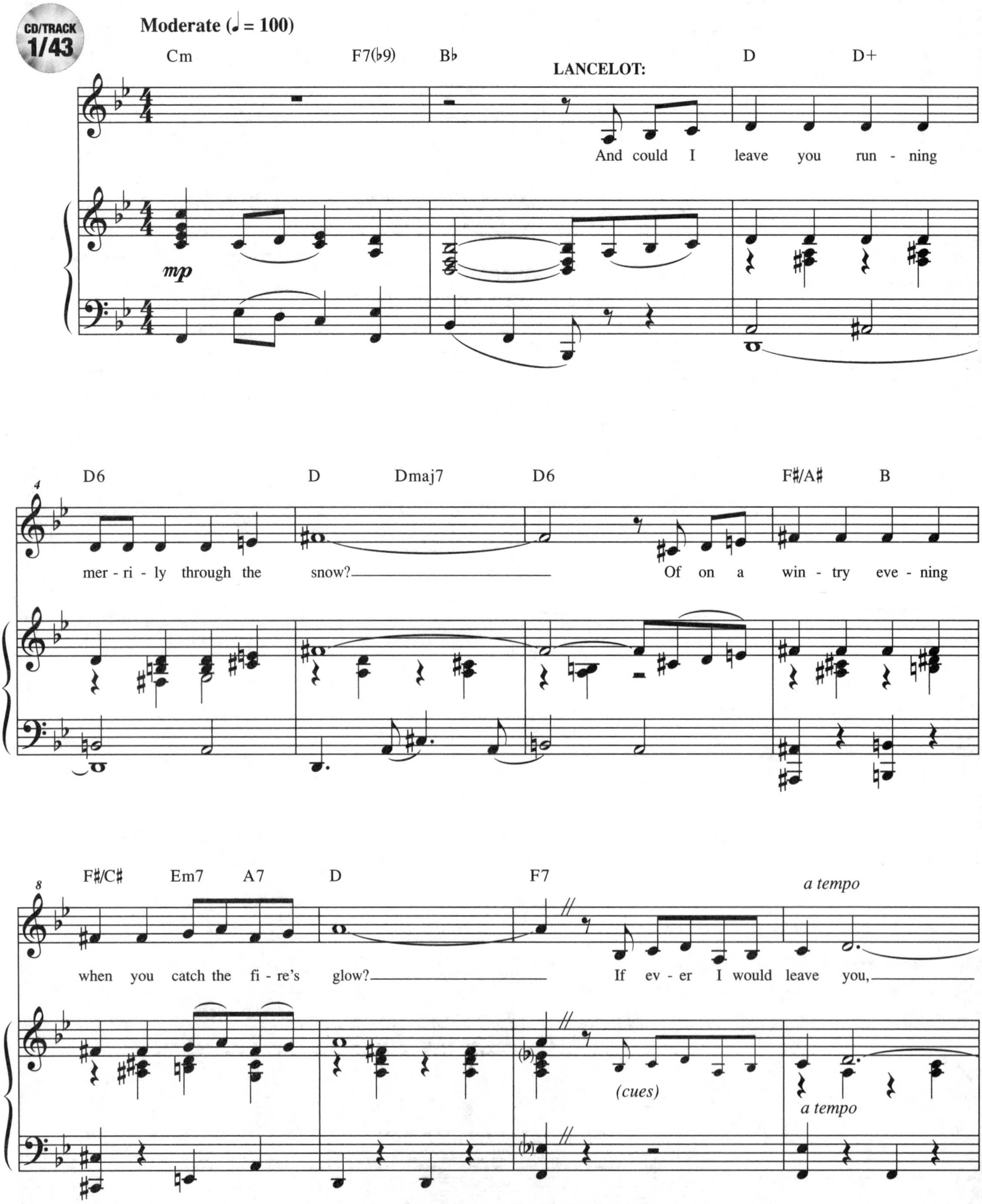

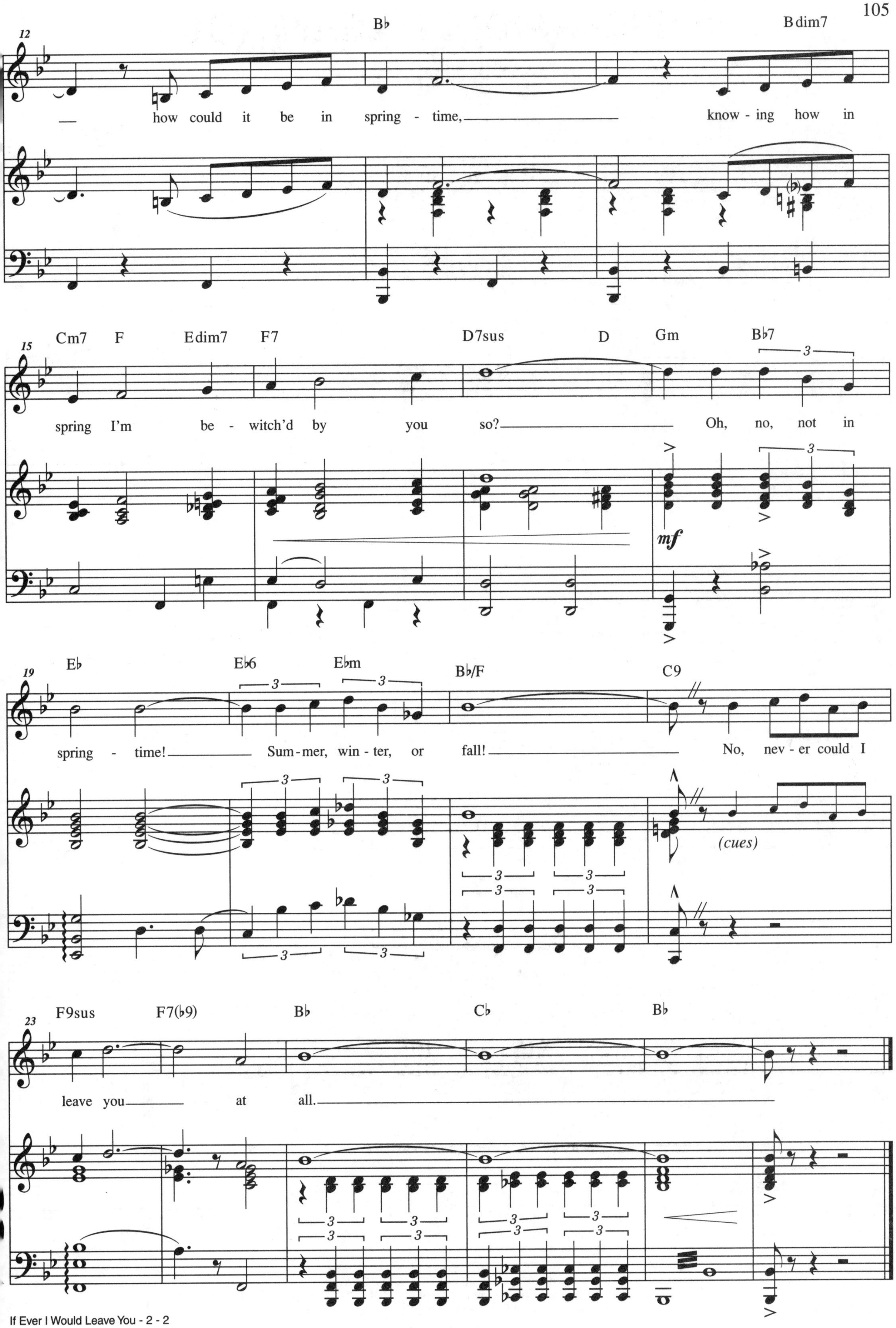
12
B♭ Bdim7
— how could it be in spring - time, know - ing how in
15
Cm7 F Edim7 F7 D7sus D Gm B♭7
spring I'm be - witch'd by you so? Oh, no, not in
mf
19
E♭ E♭6 E♭m B♭/F C9
spring - time! Sum - mer, win - ter, or fall! No, nev - er could I
(cues)
23
F9sus F7(♭9) B♭ C♭ B♭
leave you at all.

IF I ONLY HAD A BRAIN

(from "The Wizard of Oz")

Lyrics by
E. Y. HARBURG

Music by
HAROLD ARLEN

CD/TRACK 1/44

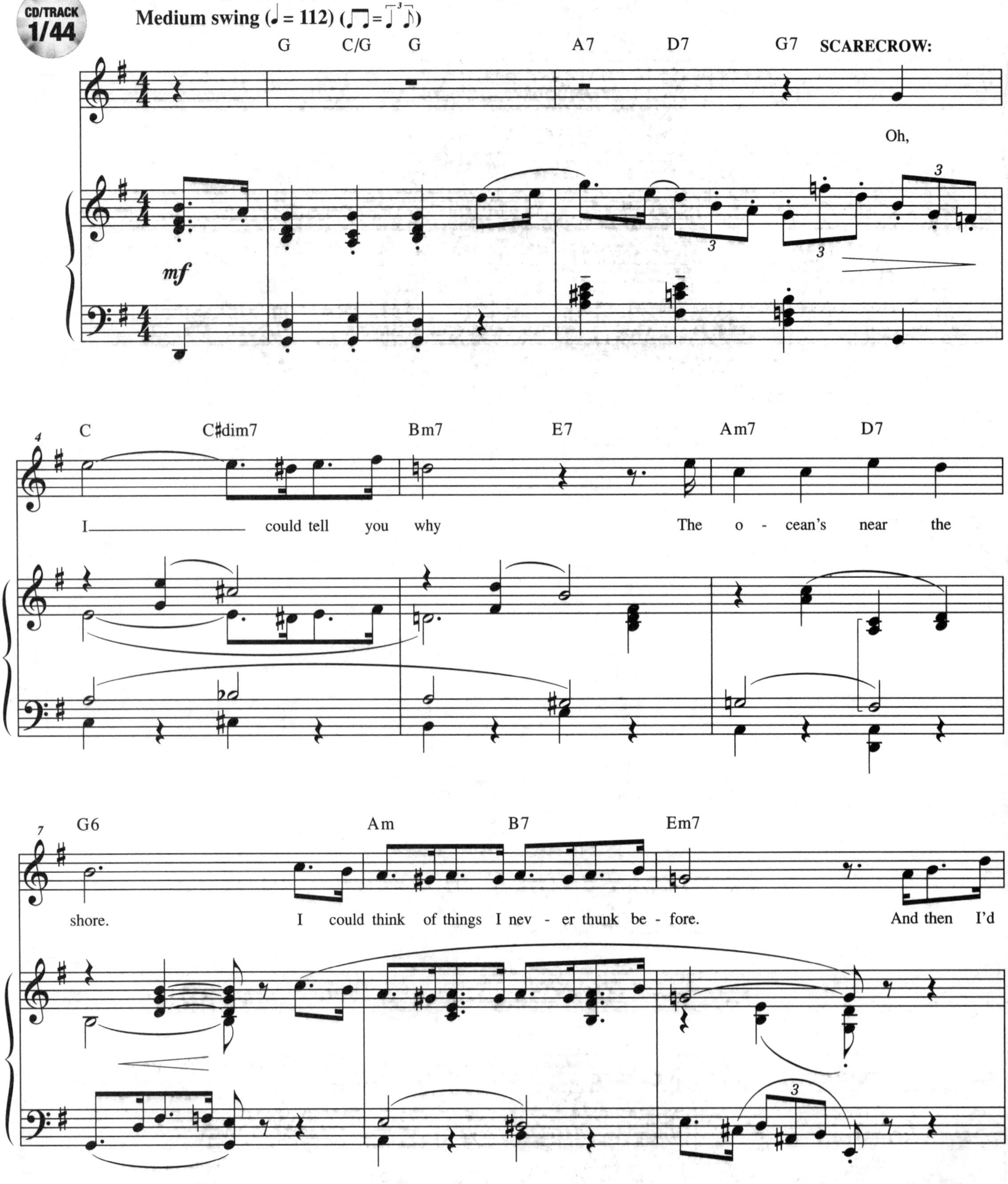

10
A7
Fdim7 D7/F♯ D7
mf
G
Am7/D
sit and think some more. Gosh, it would be aw - ful pleas-in', To
fp f mf
3
13
G6
Am6/D
Gmaj7 C6/G Gmaj7
G6
rea - son out the rea - son For things I can't ex - plain. Then per-
3
16
Am7
D7
rall.
G C/G G
a tempo
haps I'd de - serve ya, And be ev - en worth - y erve ya, If I on - ly had a brain.
rall.
a tempo
sf

IF THIS ISN'T LOVE

(from "Finian's Rainbow")

Words by
E.Y. HARBURG

Music by
BURTON LANE

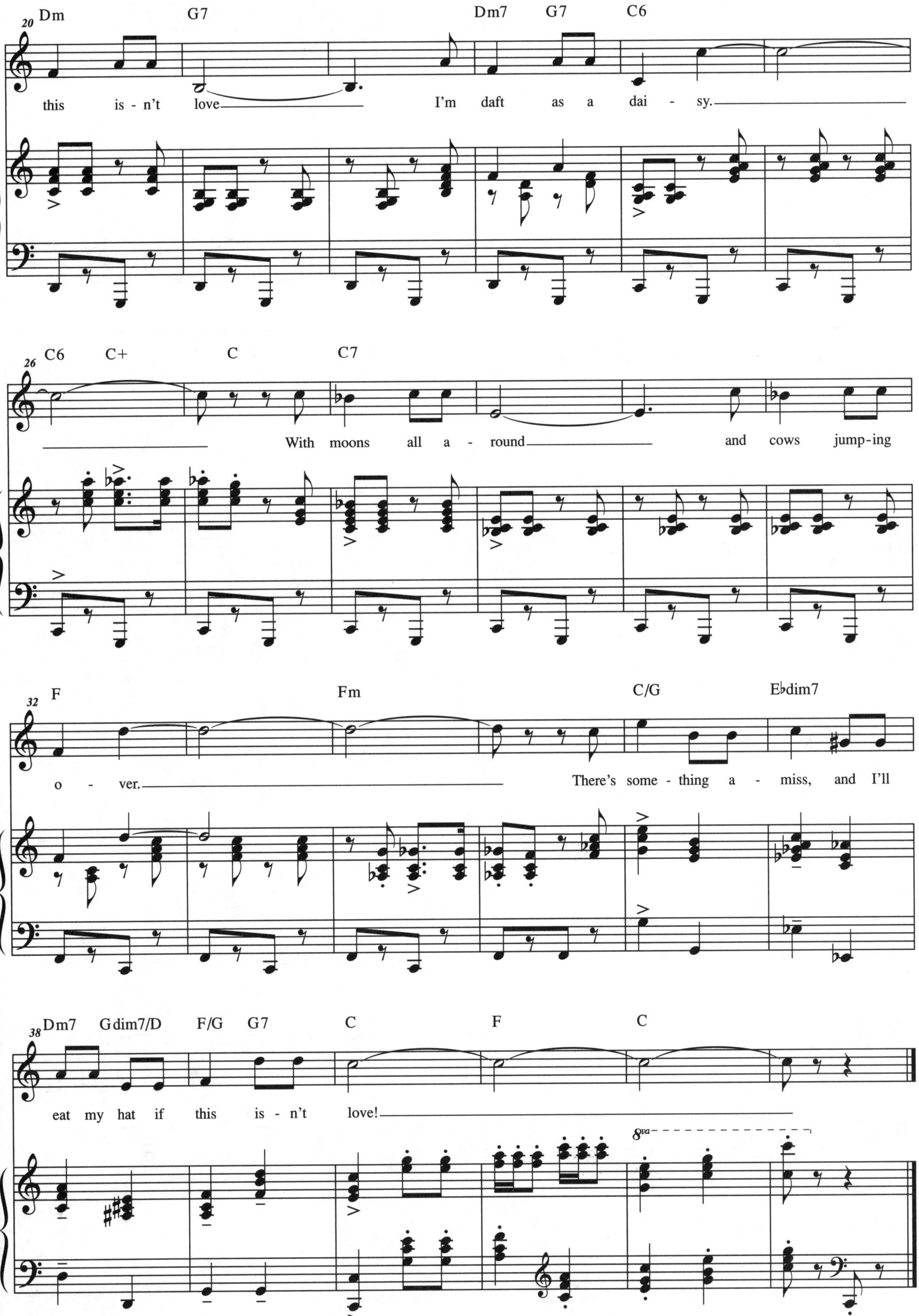
20 Dm G7 Dm7 G7 C6
this is - n't love I'm daft as a dai - sy.
26 C6 C+ C C7
With moons all a - round and cows jump - ing
32 F Fm C/G E♭dim7
o - ver. There's some - thing a - miss, and I'll
38 Dm7 Gdim7/D F/G G7 C F C
eat my hat if this is - n't love!
8va

IF YOU CAN FIND ME, I'M HERE

(from "Evening Primrose")

Music and Lyrics by
STEPHEN SONDHEIM

CD/TRACK
1/46

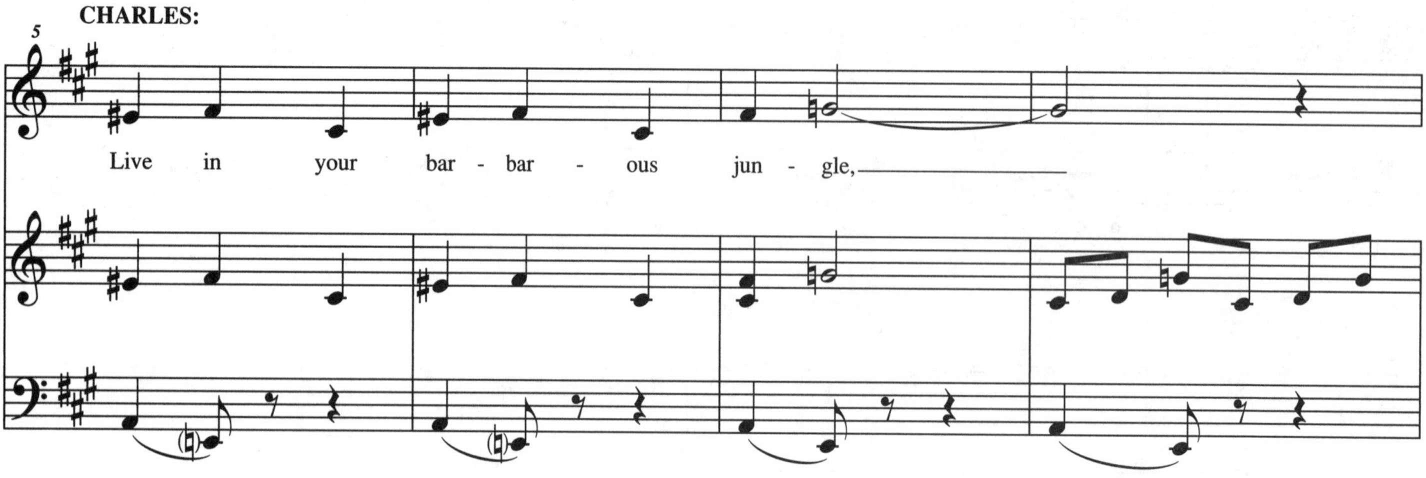

13
When all the scream - ing has died a - way, come and
18
vis - it my hide - a - way. I will be glad to pro - vide a
24
way. If you can find me, I'm here!
3xs
sub. p
mf
30
I am here!

IN A LITTLE WHILE

(from "Once Upon a Mattress")

Lyrics by
MARSHALL BARER

Music by
MARY RODGERS

CD/TRACK 1/47

Moderate, with lilt (♩ = 120)

13
B♭7/F B♭7 E♭maj7 E♭maj7/B♭ B♭m11 Gm7 C7
way I have it planned. But I'll on - ly stay in love if the
17
F7sus F7 A♭/B♭ B♭7(♯11) E♭maj7
glove con-tains your hand. I can see it all, down to ev - 'ry small de -
21
Bm7(♭5) E7 Am7(♭5) A♭m6 E♭/B♭ E♭+/F
tail. So I wish you'd look a - round un - til you've found a
24
A♭maj7 Adim B♭7sus B♭7 E♭ B♭9 E♭6
cas - tle in the neigh - bor - hood for sale.

INTO THE FIRE

(from "The Scarlet Pimpernel")

Words by
NAN KNIGHTON

Music by
FRANK WILDHORN

CD/TRACK
1/48

* Alternate lower note.

IT'S GOT TO BE LOVE

(from "On Your Toes")

Words by
LORENZ HART

Music by
RICHARD RODGERS

18
Gm6/B♭ A7 D B7 F♯m7 B7 Em7 A7
bro - ken down pump. It's got to be love, It could - n't be in - di - ges - tion.
22
Em7 A7 D7 G6 Dm7 G6 C♯m7(♭5) F♯7 E/G♯ F♯7/A♯
Be - yond an - y ques - tion, I'm flut - ter - y as a dove; I've
27
Bm7 Am6 G6 A7 A♯dim7 Bm B7(♯5) E9 A+7
heard peo - ple say it's no worse than a cold but, oh, that fe - ver! I'm
31
D B7 Em7 A7 D6/9 Fdim D Fdim D
burned to a crisp, but ne - ver - the - less it's on - ly love.
8va

IT'S NO PROBLEM (Reprise)

(from "High Fidelity")

Words and Music by TOM KITT
and AMANDA GREEN

CD/TRACK 1/50

* Alternate notes.

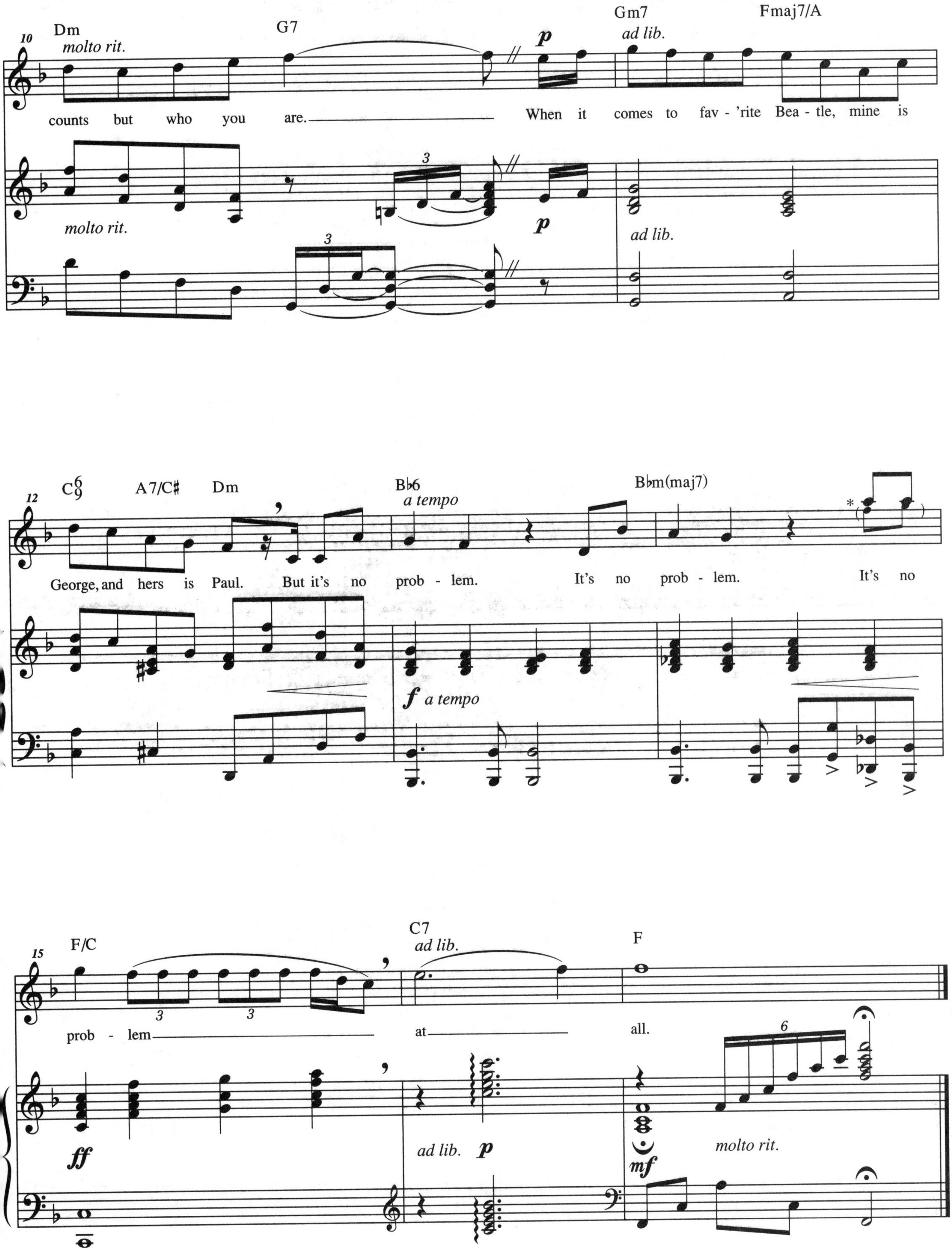
10
Dm
molto rit.
G7
Gm7
Fmaj7/A
p
ad lib.
counts but who you are.
When it comes to fav - 'rite Bea - tle, mine is
molto rit.
p
ad lib.
12
C6/9
A7/C♯
Dm
B♭6
a tempo
B♭m(maj7)
George, and hers is Paul. But it's no prob - lem. It's no prob - lem. It's no
f a tempo
15
F/C
C7
ad lib.
F
prob - lem at all.
ff
ad lib.
p
mf
molto rit.

IT'S NOT ALL RIGHT

(from "Striking 12")

Words and Music by
BRENDAN MILBURN, VALERIE VIGODA
and RACHEL SHEINKIN

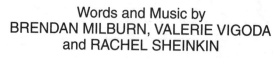

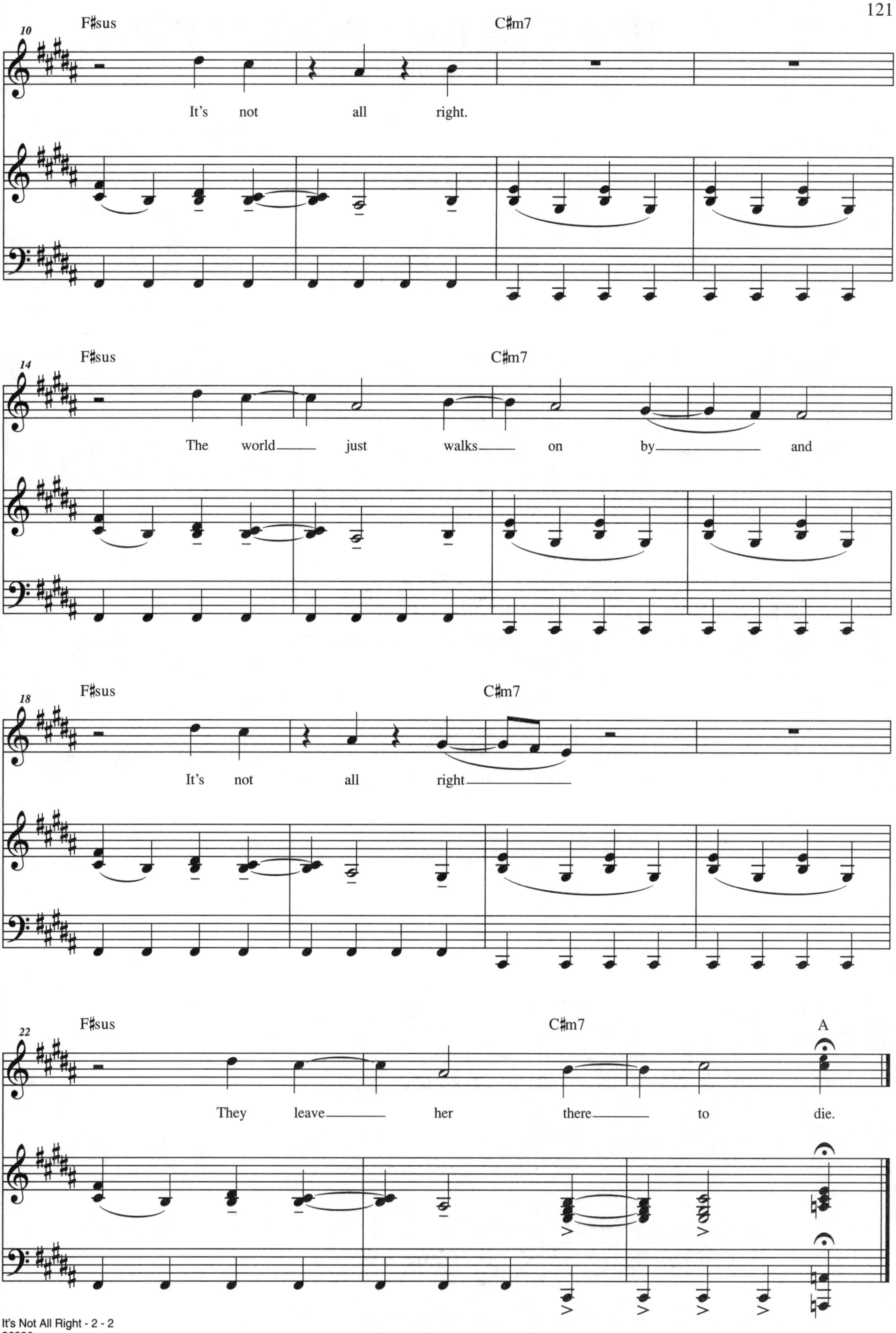
10
F♯sus
C♯m7
It's not all right.
14
F♯sus
C♯m7
The world just walks on by and
18
F♯sus
C♯m7
It's not all right
22
F♯sus
C♯m7
A
They leave her there to die.

IT'S POSSIBLE (IN McELLIGOT'S POOL)

(from "Seussical the Musical")

Lyrics by
LYNN AHRENS

Music by
STEPHEN FLAHERTY

10
G/B A D G/D D
Oh, the sea is so full of a num - ber of fish. If a
mf
13
Bm7 A A/C♯ D
fel - low is pa - tient, he might get his wish! And that's why I think that I'm
16
G/D D Bm7 A Bm D/F♯
not such a fool when I sit here and fish in Mc - El - li - got's Pool. It's
19
G D/G Em/D D
pos - si - ble. An - y - thing's pos - si - ble!
sffz
8va

JUST IN TIME
(from "Bells are Ringing")

Lyrics by
BETTY COMDEN and
ADOLPH GREEN

Music by
JULE STYNE

CD/TRACK 2/3

Moderate, 2-beat (♩ = 120)

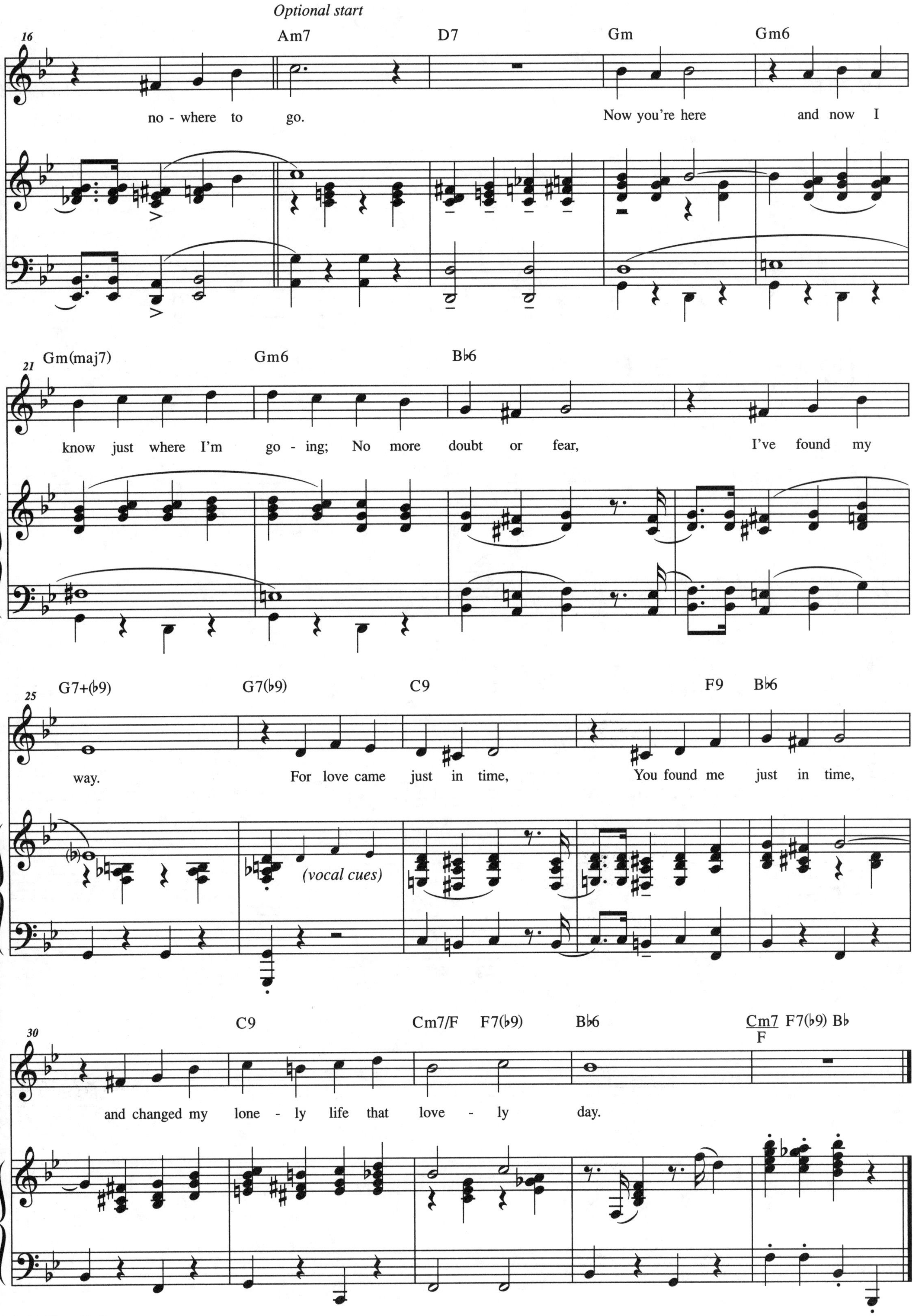
Optional start
16
Am7 D7 Gm Gm6
no - where to go. Now you're here and now I
21
Gm(maj7) Gm6 B♭6
know just where I'm go - ing; No more doubt or fear, I've found my
25
G7+(♭9) G7(♭9) C9 F9 B♭6
way. For love came just in time, You found me just in time,
(vocal cues)
30
C9 Cm7/F F7(♭9) B♭6 Cm7/F F7(♭9) B♭
and changed my lone - ly life that love - ly day.

LADIES' CHOICE
(from "Hairspray — The Movie")

Lyrics by
SCOTT WITTMAN and
MARC SHAIMAN

Music by
MARC SHAIMAN

CD/TRACK 2/4

17
D7
A7
Once you've browsed through the
20
G7
D
whole se - lec - tion, shake those hips in my di - rec - tion. Hey, lit - tle girl, on a
24
G
D
A
D7(♯9)
spend - ing spree, I don't come cheap, but the kiss - es come free. On clos - er in - spec - tion, I'm
28
G
A
G
G♯
A
D
D7(♯9)
sure that you'll a - gree.
I'm the la - dies' choice.
loco

LARGER THAN LIFE

(from "My Favorite Year")

Lyrics by
LYNN AHRENS

Music by
STEPHEN FLAHERTY

CD/TRACK
2/5

14
A♭maj9
Fm7
E♭/G
pos - si - ble fa - ther,
he stood and he fought and he
17
A♭(add9)
G/B
Cm
E♭/B♭
ne - ver ran,
oh, no.
and he
(with pedal)
21
Fm7
B♭7sus
B♭7
poco rit.
lived for me
at the R. K.
poco rit.
25
E♭
a tempo
E♭/G
A♭
B♭7sus
E♭
rit.
O.
a tempo
rit.

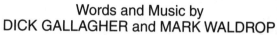

LAST ONE PICKED

(from "Howard Crabtree's Whoop-dee-doo!")

Words and Music by
DICK GALLAGHER and MARK WALDROP

CD/TRACK 2/6

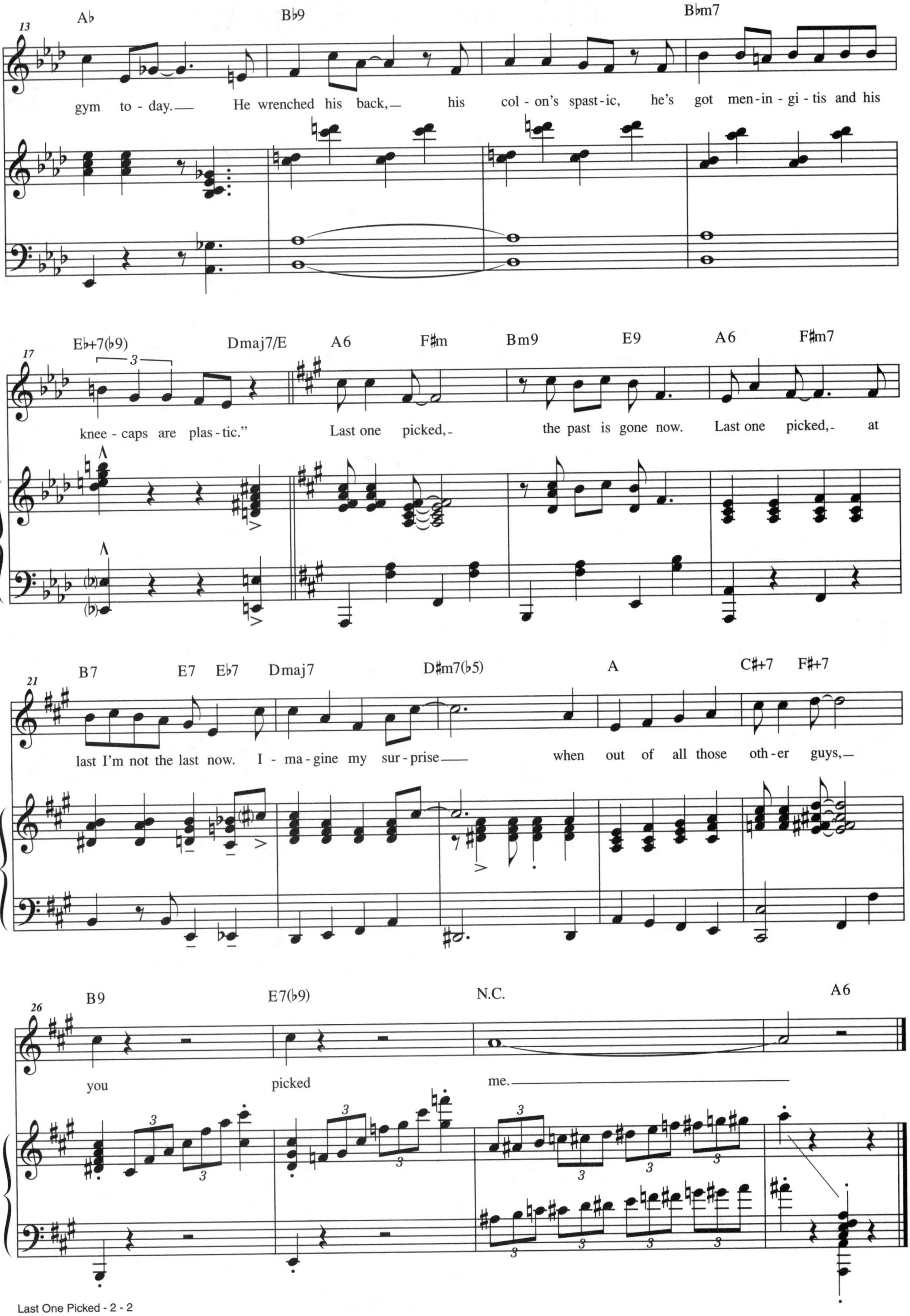
13
A♭ B♭9 B♭m7
gym to - day. He wrenched his back, his col - on's spast - ic, he's got men - in - gi - tis and his
17
E♭+7(♭9) Dmaj7/E A6 F♯m Bm9 E9 A6 F♯m7
knee - caps are plas - tic." Last one picked, the past is gone now. Last one picked, at
21
B7 E7 E♭7 Dmaj7 D♯m7(♭5) A C♯+7 F♯+7
last I'm not the last now. I - ma - gine my sur - prise when out of all those oth - er guys,
26
B9 E7(♭9) N.C. A6
you picked me.

LAY ALL YOUR LOVE ON ME

(from "Mamma Mia!")

Words and Music by
BENNY ANDERSSON
and BJORN ULVAEUS

CD/TRACK 2/7
Disco, up tempo (♩ = 132)
Fm
SKY:
I was-n't jeal - ous be - fore we met.
mf
Eb
Now ev-'ry man that I see is a po - ten-tial threat.
Fm
And I'm pos - es - sive, it is - n't nice. You've heard me say - ing that
Eb
Fm
smok - ing was my on - ly vice. But now it is - n't true,—

15
C7/E
Fm
now ev-'ry-thing_ is new_
and all I've learned_ has
19
C7/G
Fm/A♭
B♭
o - ver - turned._ I beg of you:_
23
Fm
C/F
Fm
C/F
Fm
D♭
C
Don't go wast - ing your e - mo - tion,
27
Fm
E♭/G
A♭
D♭6
E♭
A♭
lay all your love on me._

LEFT BEHIND
(from "Spring Awakening")

Lyrics by
STEVEN SATER

Music by
DUNCAN SHEIK

11
Cmaj9
still left be - hind...
It
14
A7
Cmaj9
whis - tles through the ghosts
still left be - hind...
17
Em13
It whis - tles through the ghosts
still left be -
20
poco rit.
hind...
Oh.
2
2
2
2
poco rit.

LET'S DO IT, LET'S FALL IN LOVE
(from "Paris")

Words and Music by
COLE PORTER

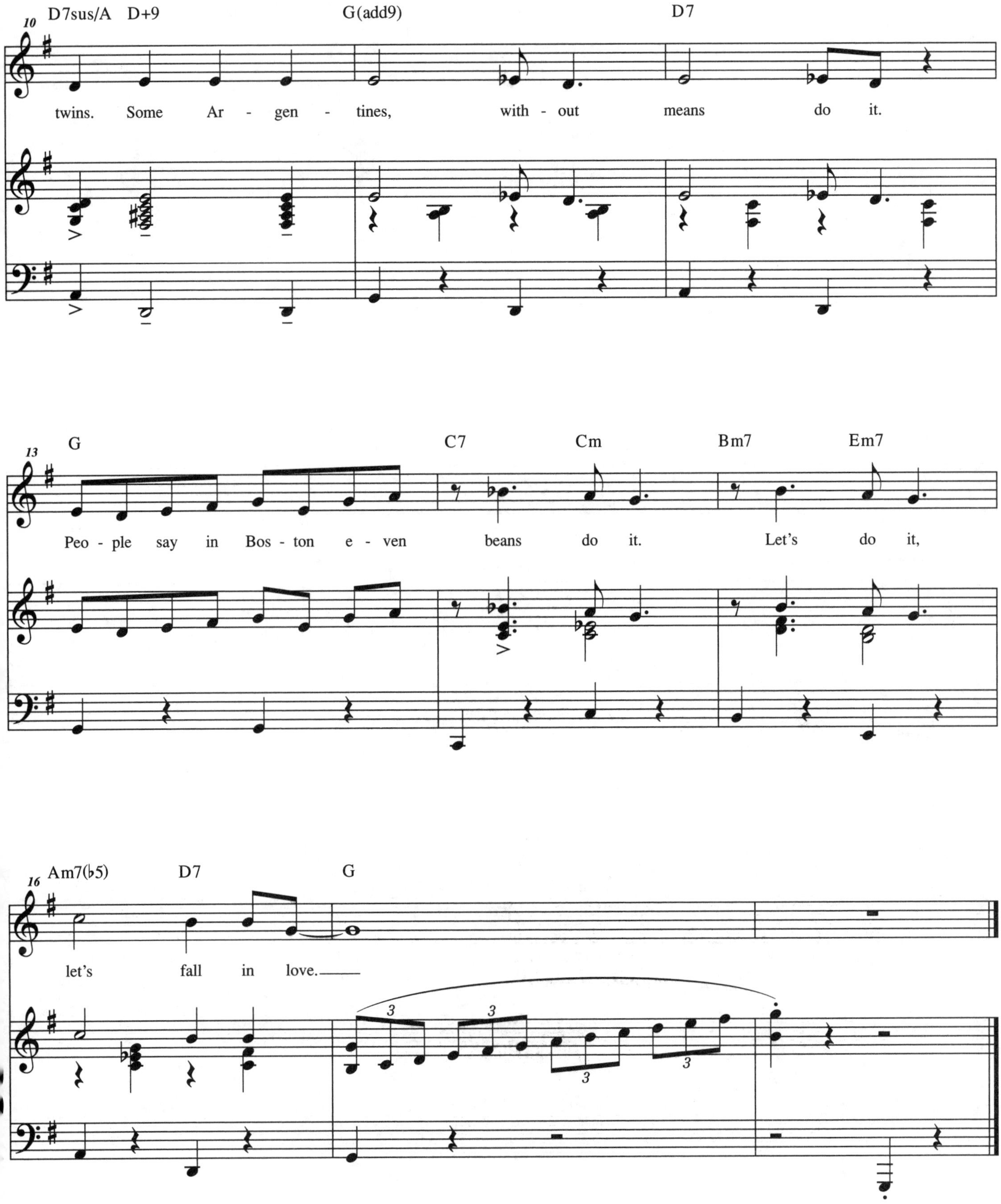
10
D7sus/A D+9 G(add9) D7
twins. Some Ar - gen - tines, with - out means do it.
13
G C7 Cm Bm7 Em7
Peo - ple say in Bos - ton e - ven beans do it. Let's do it,
16
Am7(♭5) D7 G
let's fall in love.
3
3
3
3

LILY'S EYES
(from "The Secret Garden")

Lyrics by
MARSHA NORMAN

Music by
LUCY SIMON

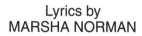

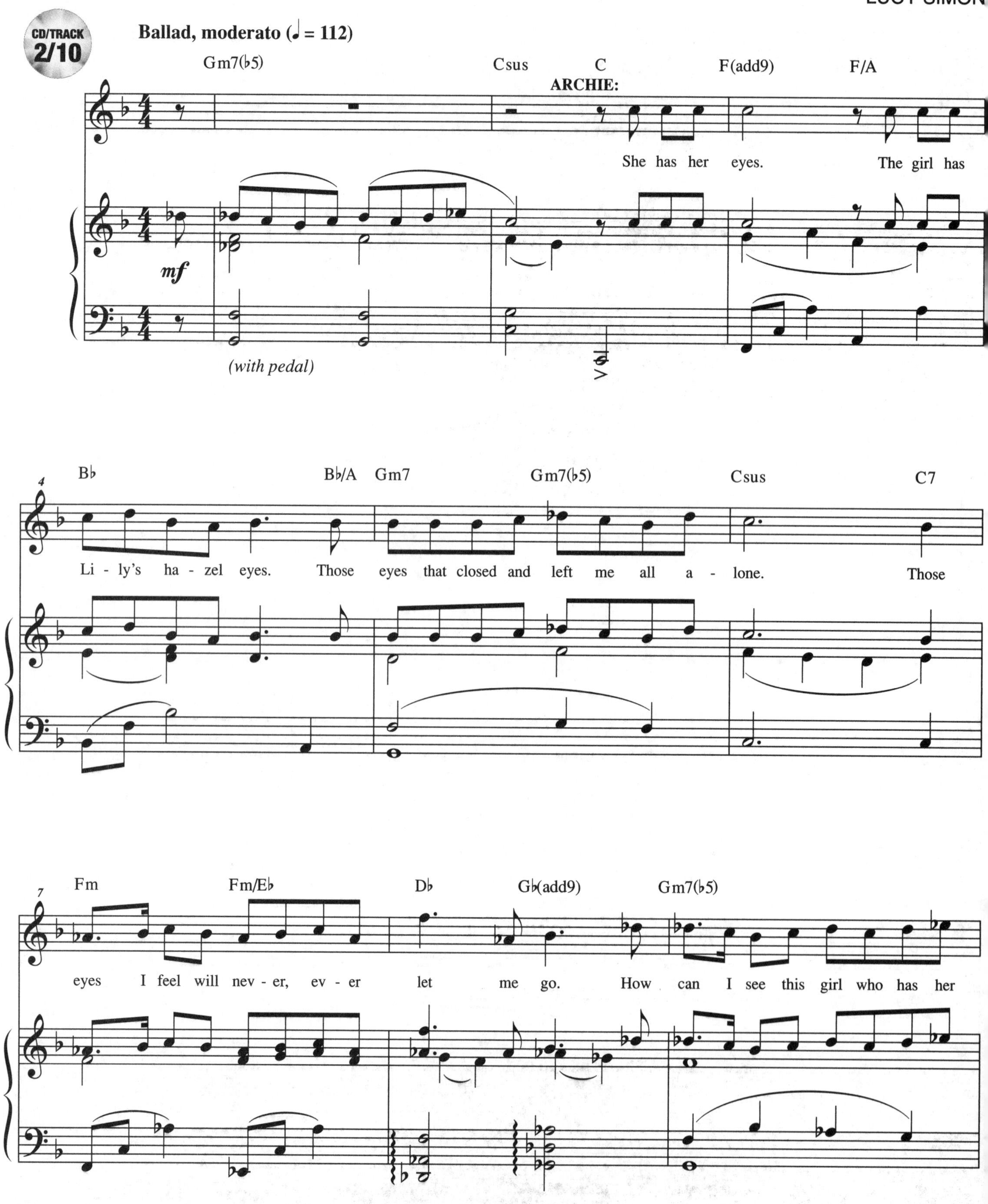

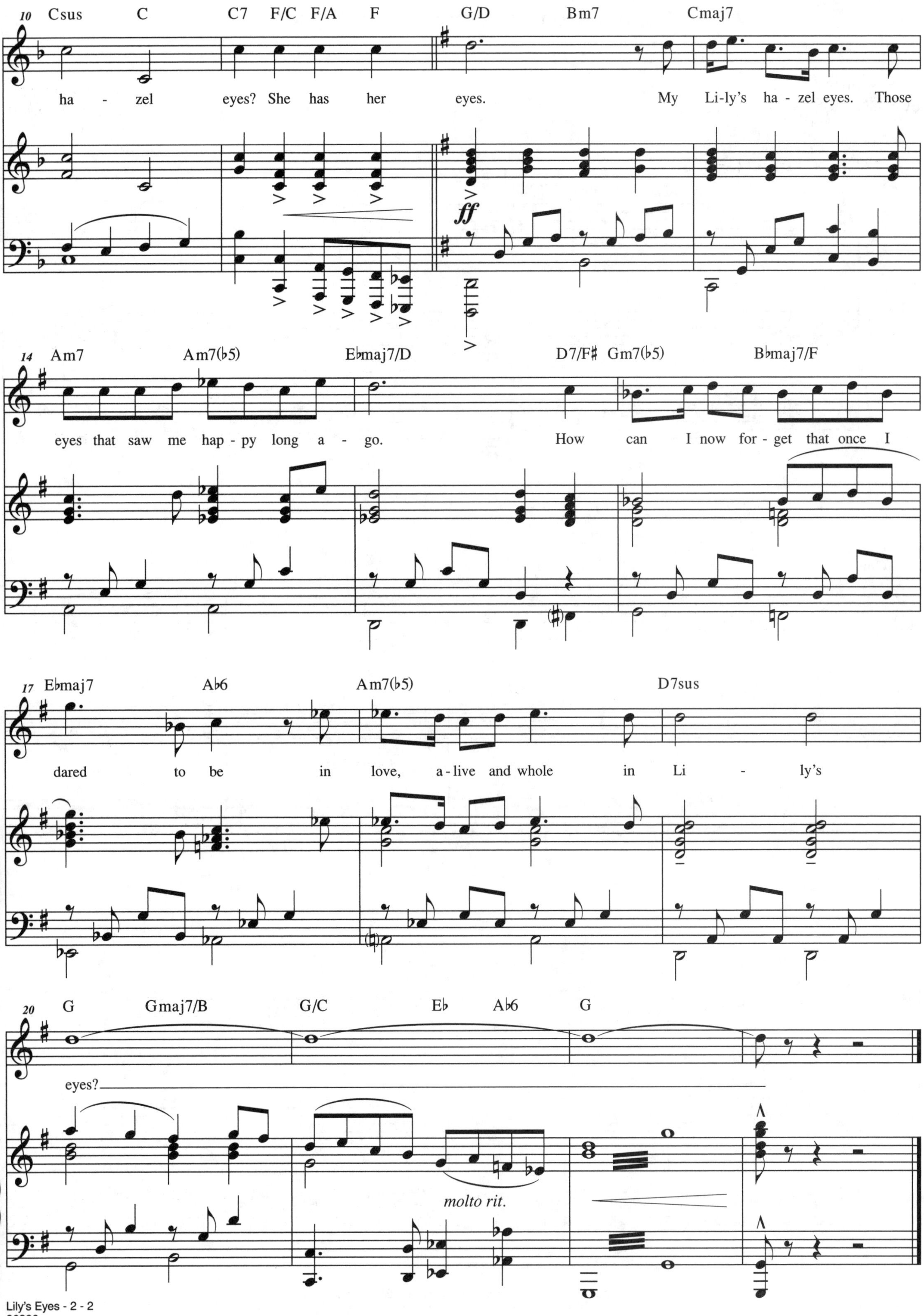
10
Csus C C7 F/C F/A F G/D Bm7 Cmaj7
ha - zel eyes? She has her eyes. My Li-ly's ha - zel eyes. Those
ff
14
Am7 Am7(♭5) E♭maj7/D D7/F♯ Gm7(♭5) B♭maj7/F
eyes that saw me hap - py long a - go. How can I now for - get that once I
17
E♭maj7 A♭6 Am7(♭5) D7sus
dared to be in love, a - live and whole in Li - ly's
20
G Gmaj7/B G/C E♭ A♭6 G
eyes?
molto rit.

LONESOME POLECAT
(from "Seven Brides for Seven Brothers")

Words by
JOHNNY MERCER

Music by
GENE de PAUL

CD/TRACK 2/11

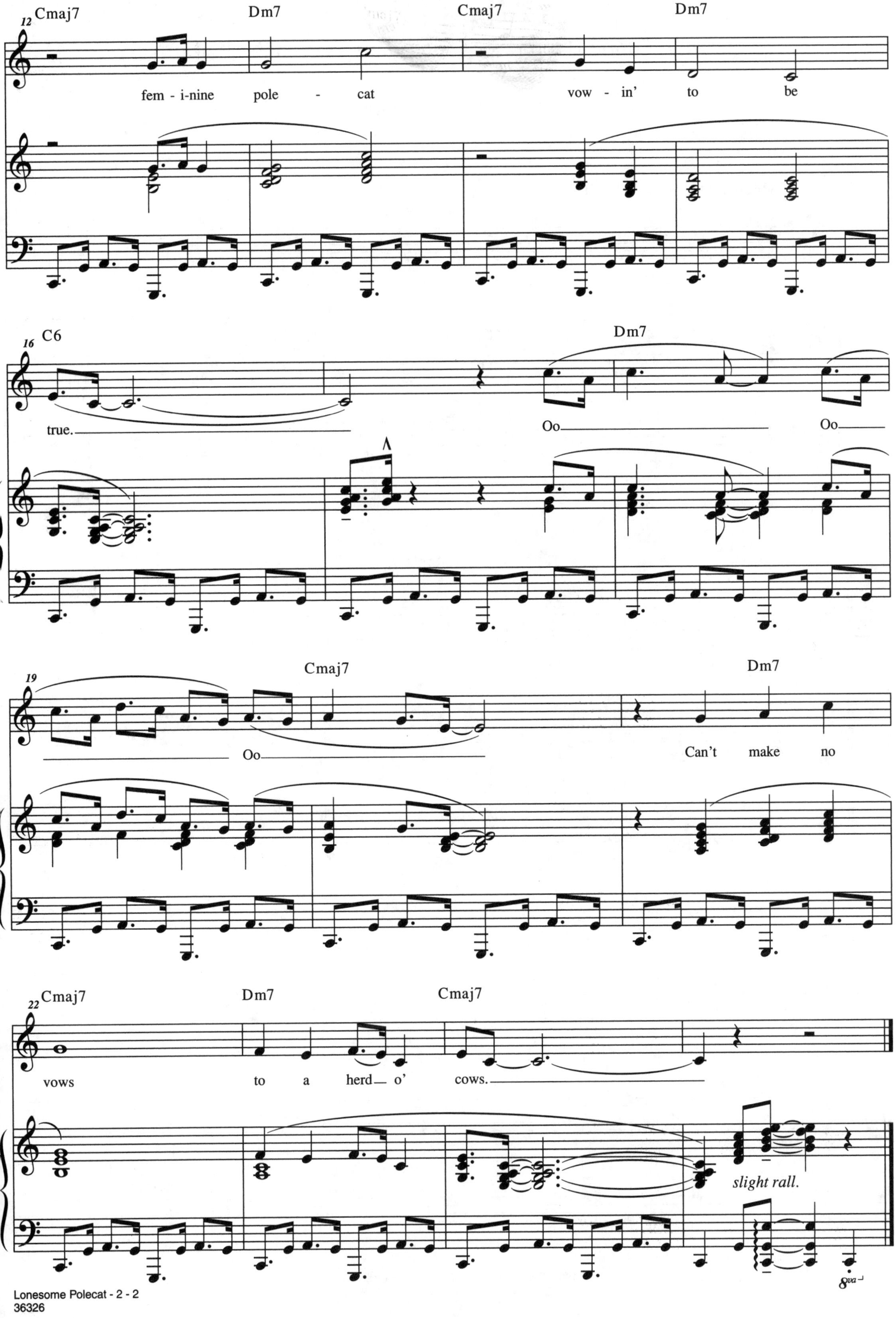
12
Cmaj7
Dm7
Cmaj7
Dm7
fem - i-nine pole - cat vow - in' to be
16
C6
Dm7
true.
Oo
Oo
19
Cmaj7
Dm7
Oo
Can't make no
22
Cmaj7
Dm7
Cmaj7
vows to a herd o' cows.
slight rall.
8va

LOVE, I HEAR

(from "A Funny Thing Happened on the Way to the Forum")

Music and Lyrics by
STEPHEN SONDHEIM

CD/TRACK 2/12

Moderately, in 4 (♩ = 132)

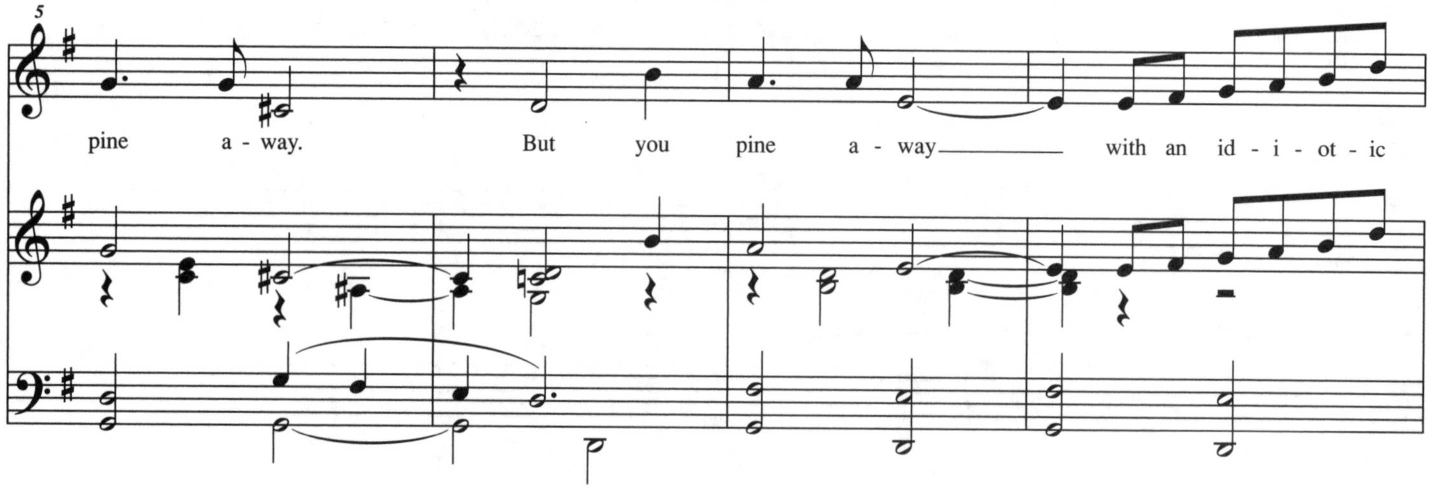

13
poco accel.
nev - er felt so well be - fore! What's love, I hear, I feel, I fear, I
cresc.
poco accel.
17
cresc.
know I am, I'm sure... I mean... I hope, I trust... I pray... I must be
cresc.
21
in!
f
(with pedal)
8va

LUCKY TO BE ME

(from "On the Town")

Lyrics by
BETTY COMDEN and ADOLPH GREEN

Music by
LEONARD BERNSTEIN

CD/TRACK 2/13

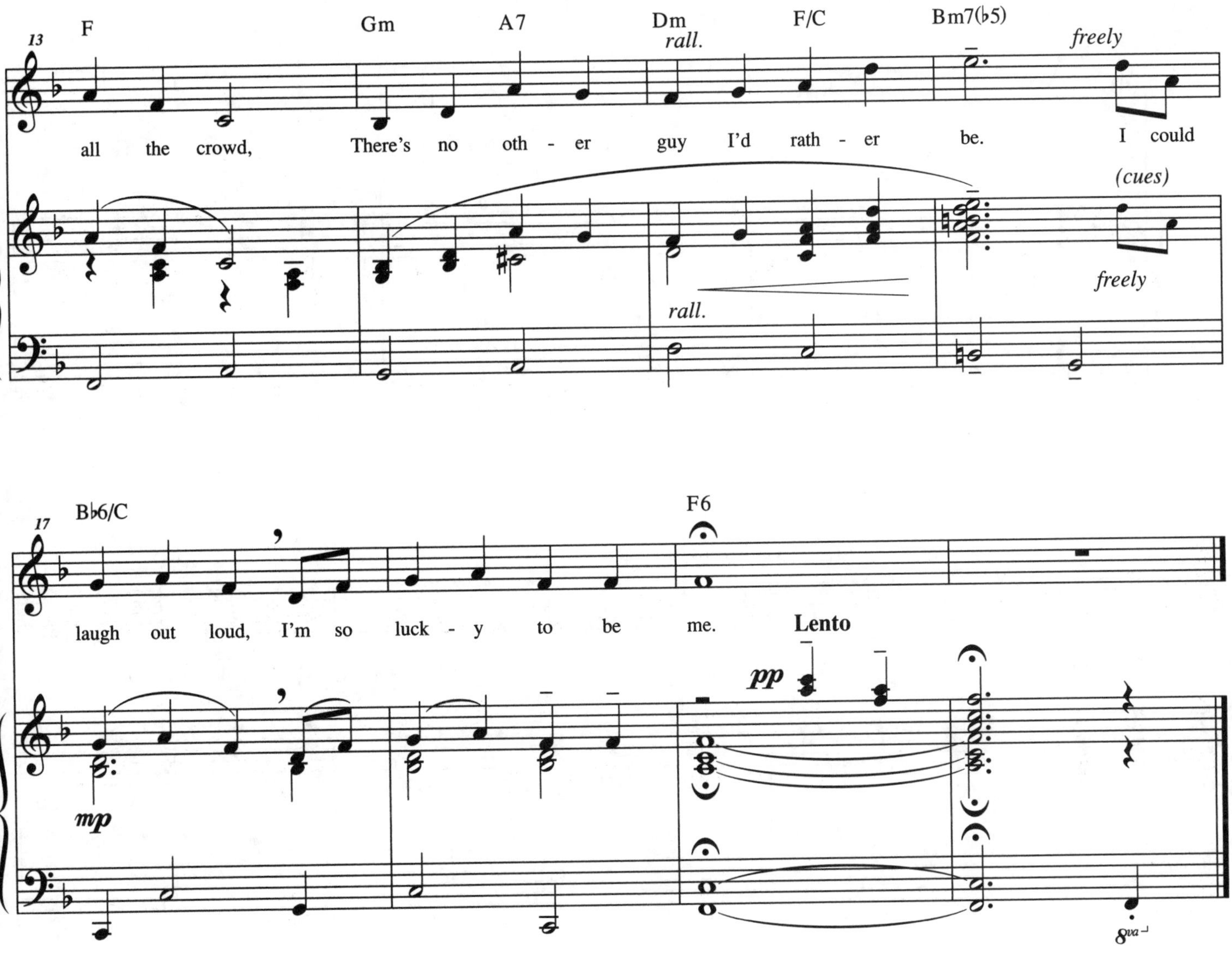
13
F
Gm
A7
Dm
F/C
Bm7(♭5)
rall.
freely
all the crowd, There's no oth - er guy I'd rath - er be. I could
(cues)
freely
rall.
17
B♭6/C
F6
laugh out loud, I'm so luck - y to be me.
Lento
pp
mp
8va

MISTER CELLOPHANE

(from "Chicago")

Words by
FRED EBB

Music by
JOHN KANDER

CD/TRACK
2/14

Slow rag, with extended accelerando and crescendo

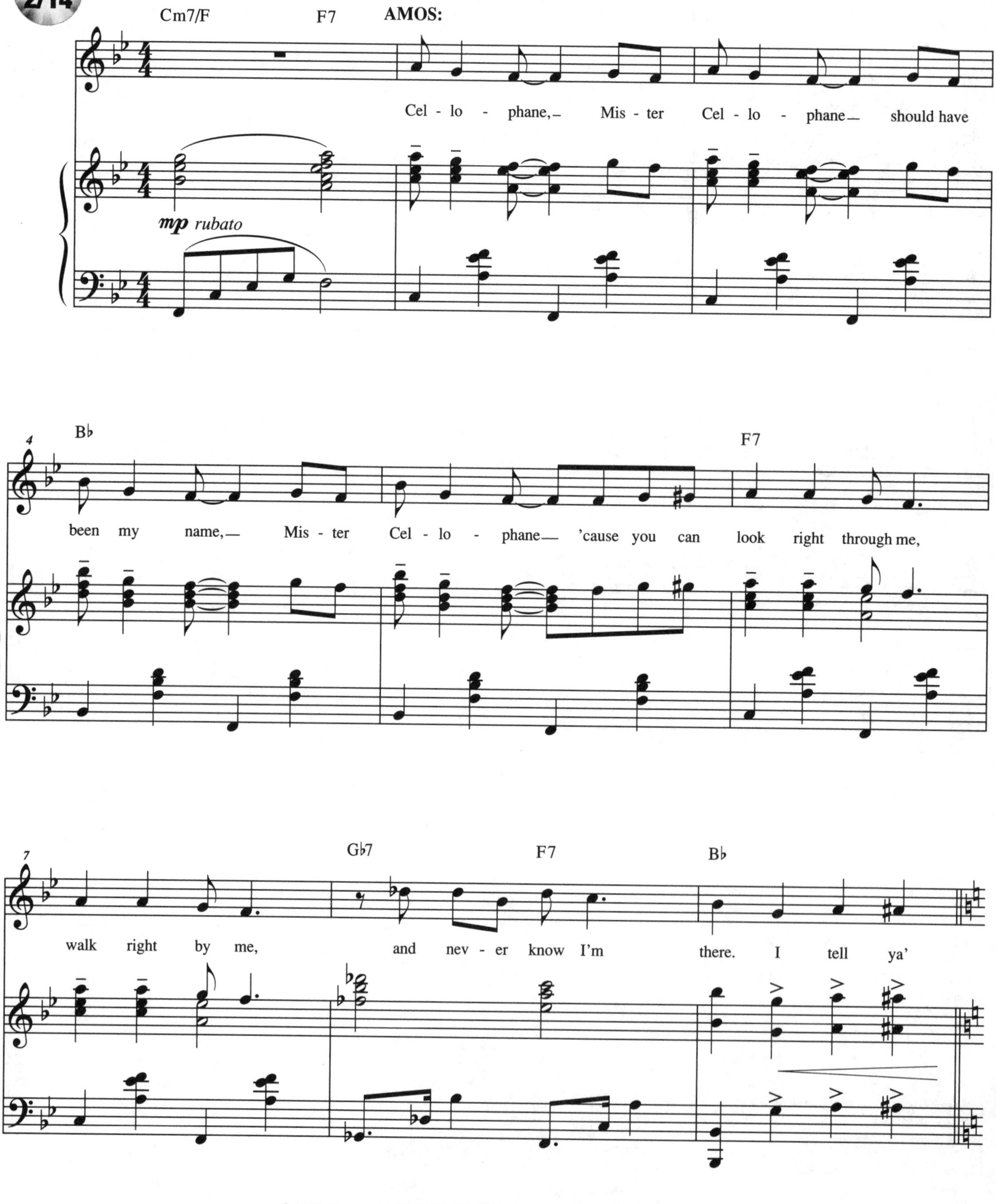

In strict tempo (♩ = 88)

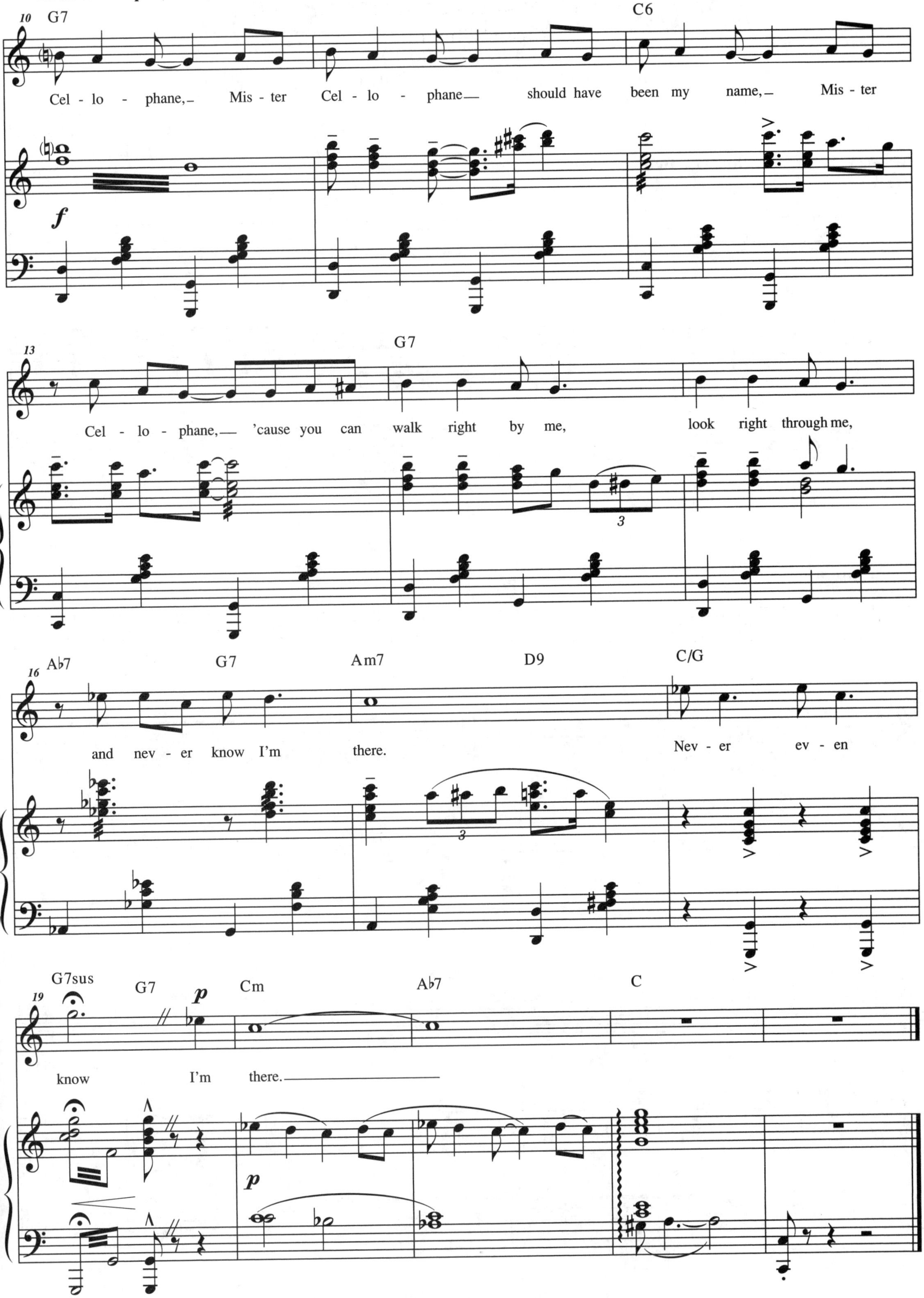

MY UNFORTUNATE ERECTION

(Chip's Lament)
(from "The 25th Annual Putnam County Spelling Bee")

Words and Music by
WILLIAM FINN

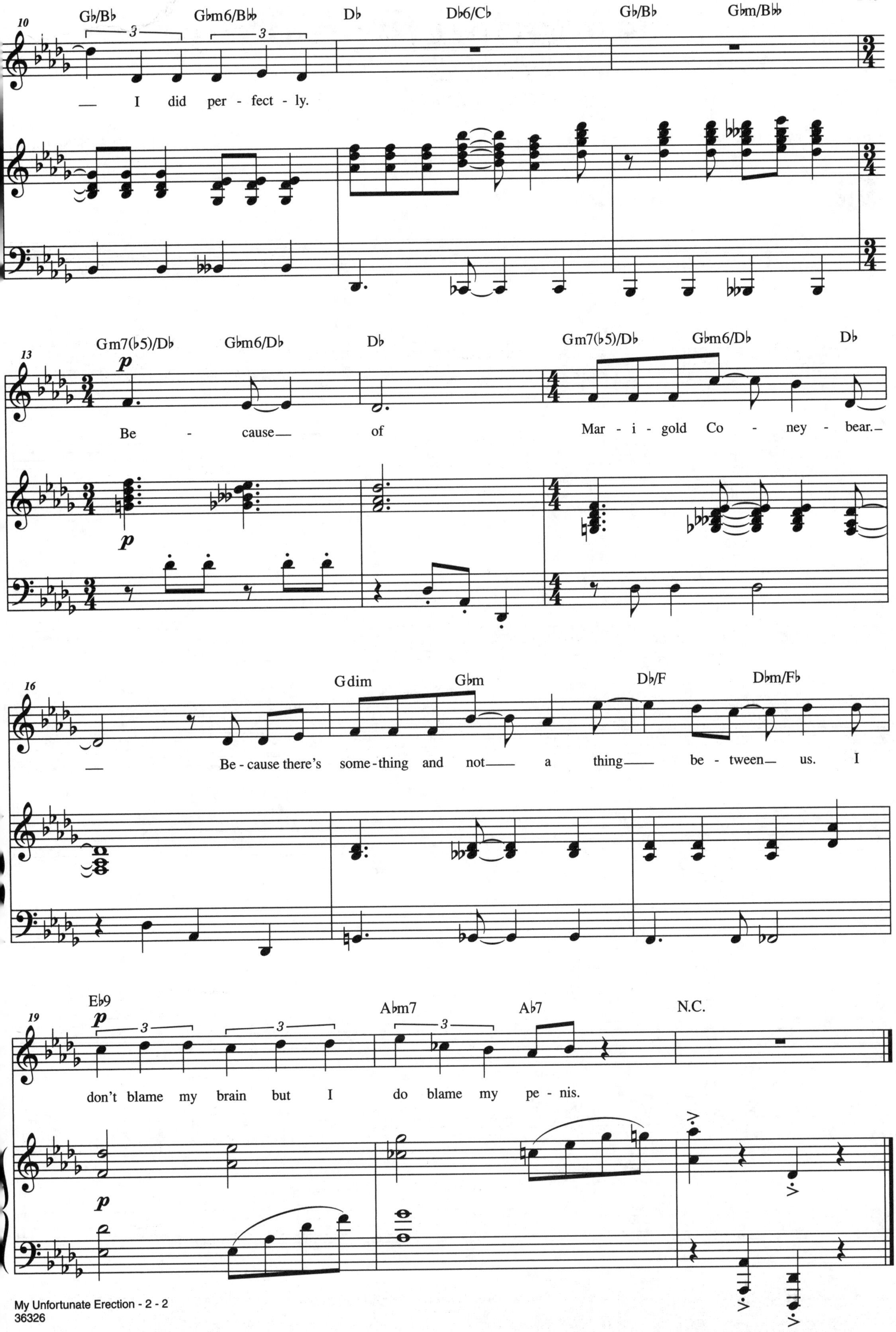
10
G♭/B♭ Gbm6/B♭♭ D♭ D♭6/C♭ G♭/B♭ G♭m/B♭♭
— I did per - fect - ly.
13
Gm7(♭5)/D♭ G♭m6/D♭ D♭ Gm7(♭5)/D♭ G♭m6/D♭ D♭
p
Be - cause — of Mar - i - gold Co - ney - bear. —
p
16
Gdim G♭m D♭/F D♭m/F♭
— Be - cause there's some - thing and not — a thing — be - tween — us. I
19
E♭9 A♭m7 A♭7 N.C.
p
don't blame my brain but I do blame my pe - nis.
p

NEW YORK, NEW YORK
(from "On the Town")

Lyrics by
BETTY COMDEN and ADOLPH GREEN

Music by
LEONARD BERNSTEIN

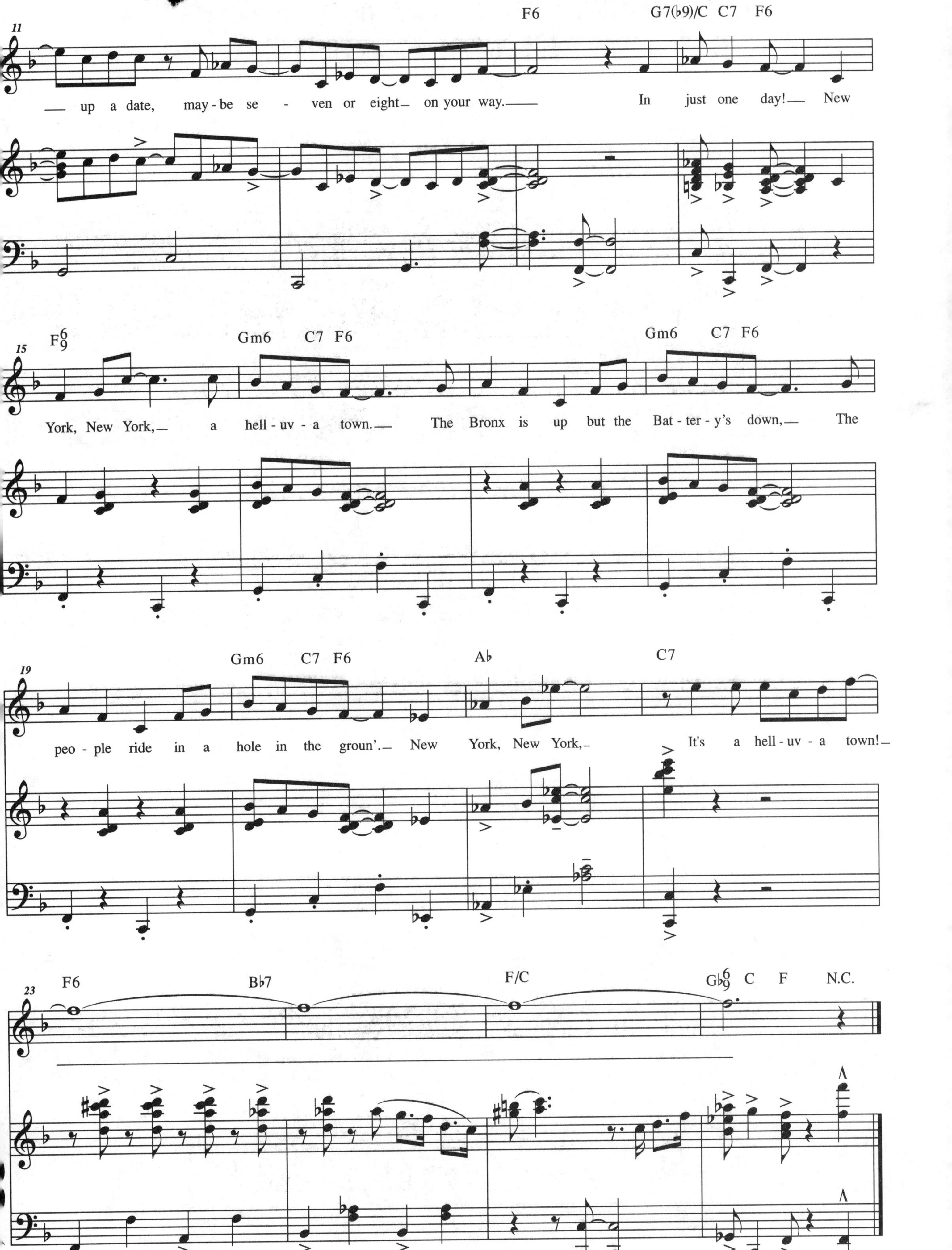
11
F6 G7(♭9)/C C7 F6
— up a date, may - be se - ven or eight — on your way. — In just one day! — New
15
F6/9 Gm6 C7 F6 Gm6 C7 F6
York, New York, — a hell - uv - a town. — The Bronx is up but the Bat - ter - y's down, — The
19
Gm6 C7 F6 A♭ C7
peo - ple ride in a hole in the groun'. — New York, New York, — It's a hell - uv - a town! —
23
F6 B♭7 F/C G♭6/9 C F N.C.

THE NIGHT THAT GOLDMAN SPOKE AT UNION SQUARE

(from "Ragtime")

Lyrics by
LYNN AHRENS

Music by
STEPHEN FLAHERTY

CD/TRACK 2/17

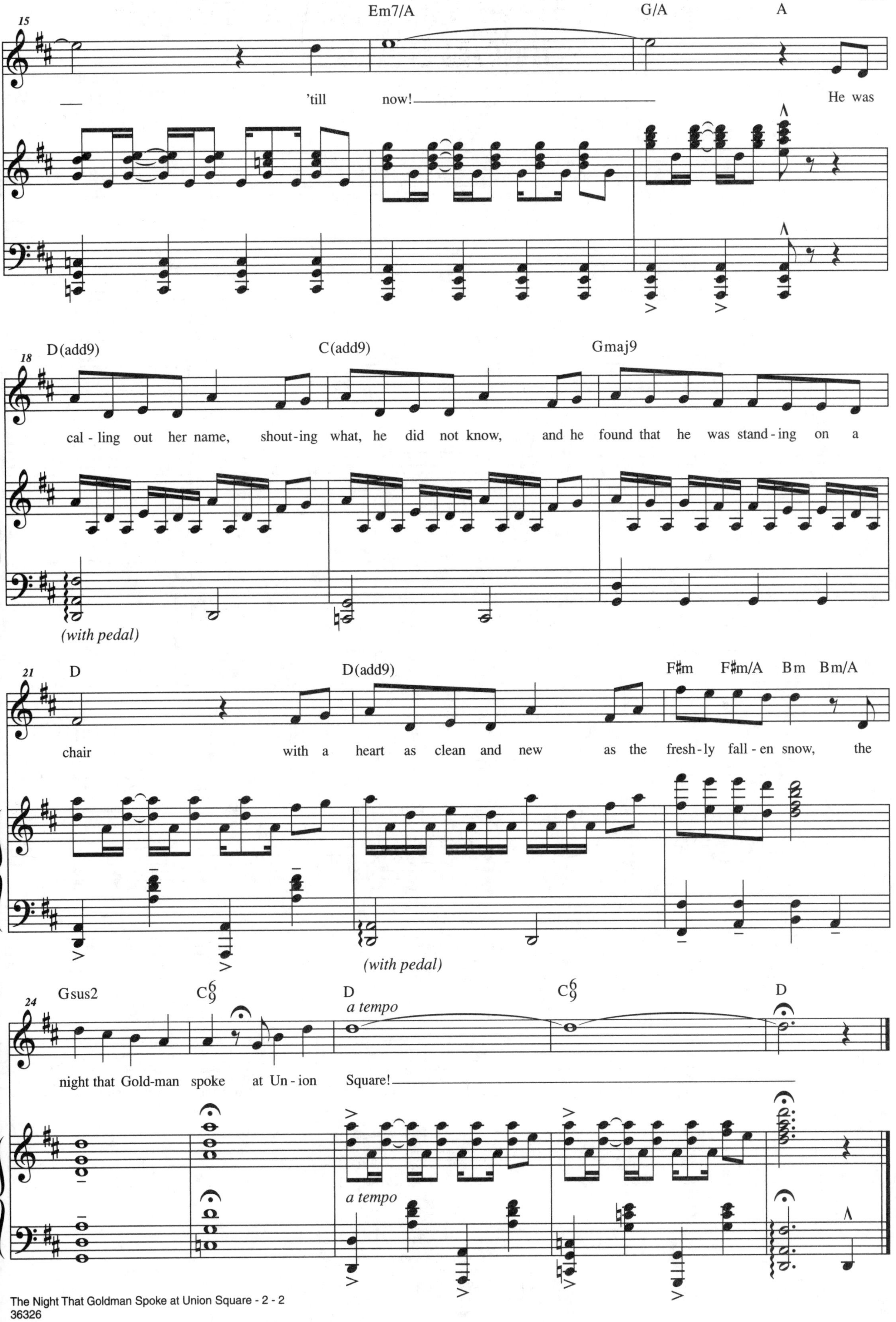
15
Em7/A
G/A
A
'till now!
He was
18
D(add9)
C(add9)
Gmaj9
cal - ling out her name, shout-ing what, he did not know, and he found that he was stand-ing on a
(with pedal)
21
D
D(add9)
F♯m F♯m/A Bm Bm/A
chair with a heart as clean and new as the fresh-ly fall - en snow, the
(with pedal)
24
Gsus2
C6/9
D
a tempo
C6/9
D
night that Gold-man spoke at Un - ion Square!
a tempo

ON THE STREET WHERE YOU LIVE

(from "My Fair Lady")

Words by
ALAN JAY LERNER

Music by
FREDERICK LOEWE

19
G13 Cmaj7 G7 Cmaj7
They don't both - er me, for there's no - where else on
23
E♭dim7 D13 G9 Dm Gdim7 Dm9
earth that I would rath - er be. Let the time go by;
cresc.
27
Dm7(♭5) G6 Am7/G D9
I won't care if I can be here on the
31
G9 F/G G7 C Am F C
street where you live.
ff
pp

PERFECT FOR YOU

(from "Next to Normal")

Lyrics by
BRIAN YORKEY

Music by
TOM KITT

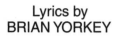

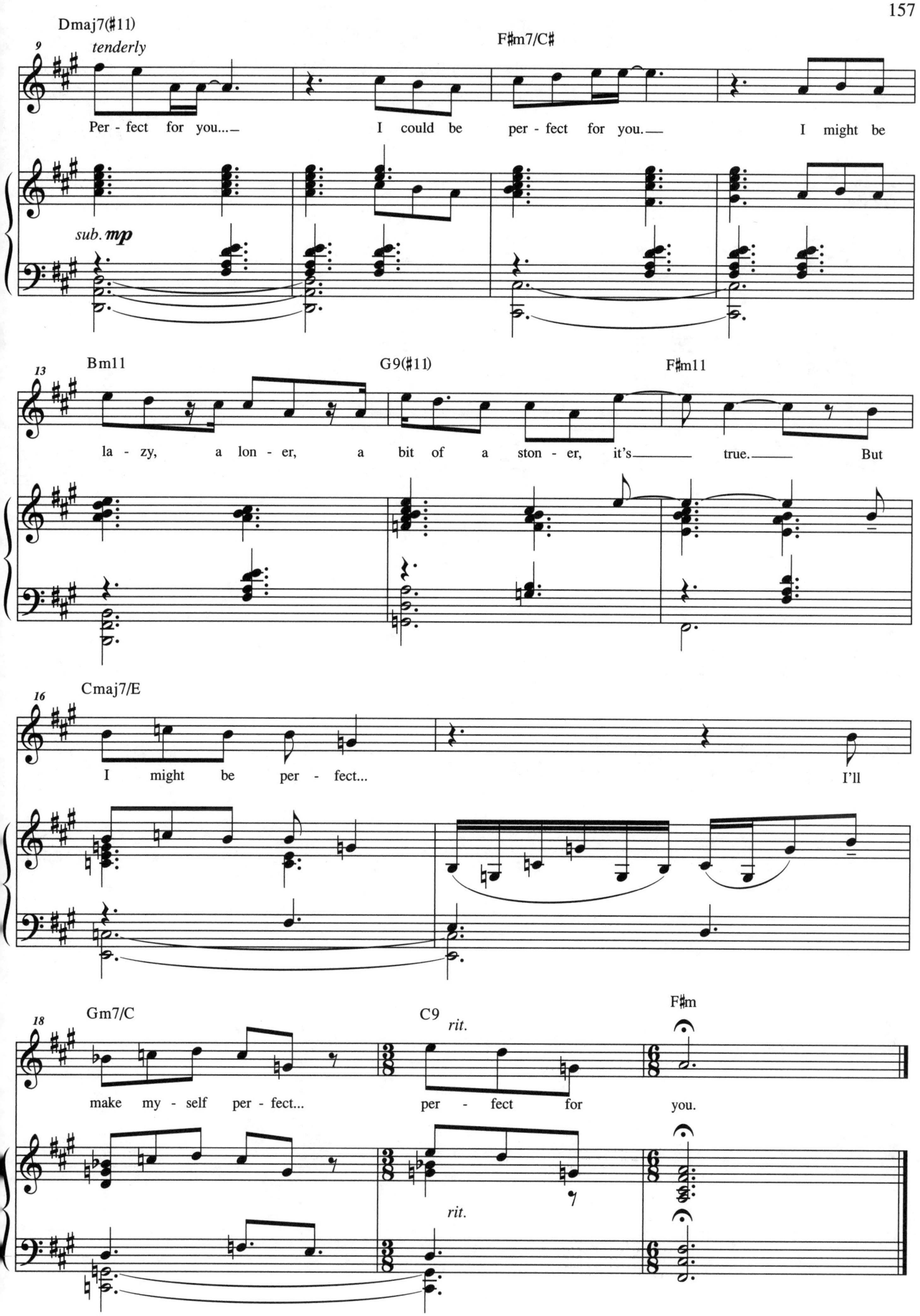
Dmaj7(#11)
tenderly
F#m7/C#
Per - fect for you... I could be per - fect for you. I might be
sub. mp
Bm11
G9(#11)
F#m11
la - zy, a lon - er, a bit of a ston - er, it's true. But
Cmaj7/E
I might be per - fect... I'll
Gm7/C
C9
rit.
F#m
make my - self per - fect... per - fect for you.
rit.

THE PROPOSAL

(from "Titanic: A New Musical")

Music and Lyrics by
MAURY YESTON

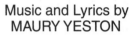

CD/TRACK 2/20

With movement **In 2 (𝅗𝅥 = 63)**

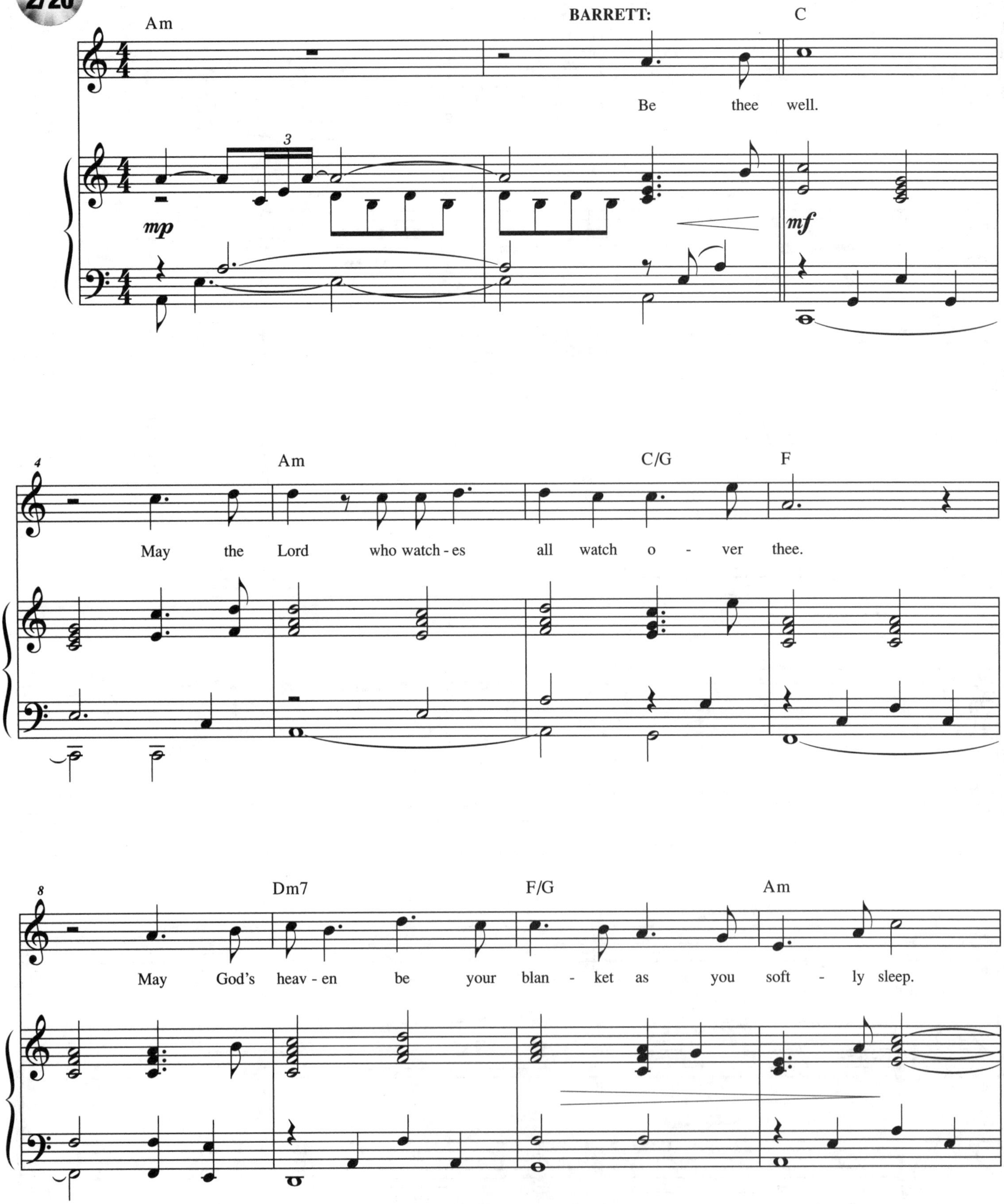

12
C
Am
Mar - ry me!
When you're fi - n'lly in my
f
16
C/G
F
arms you'll plain - ly see
this de -
mp
19 Dm7
F/G
Am
-vot - ed sail - or's heart and soul are yours to keep,
23 G
Am
yours to keep...
p rit.

THE RAIN SONG

(from "110 in the Shade")

Words by
TOM JONES

Music by
HARVEY SCHMIDT

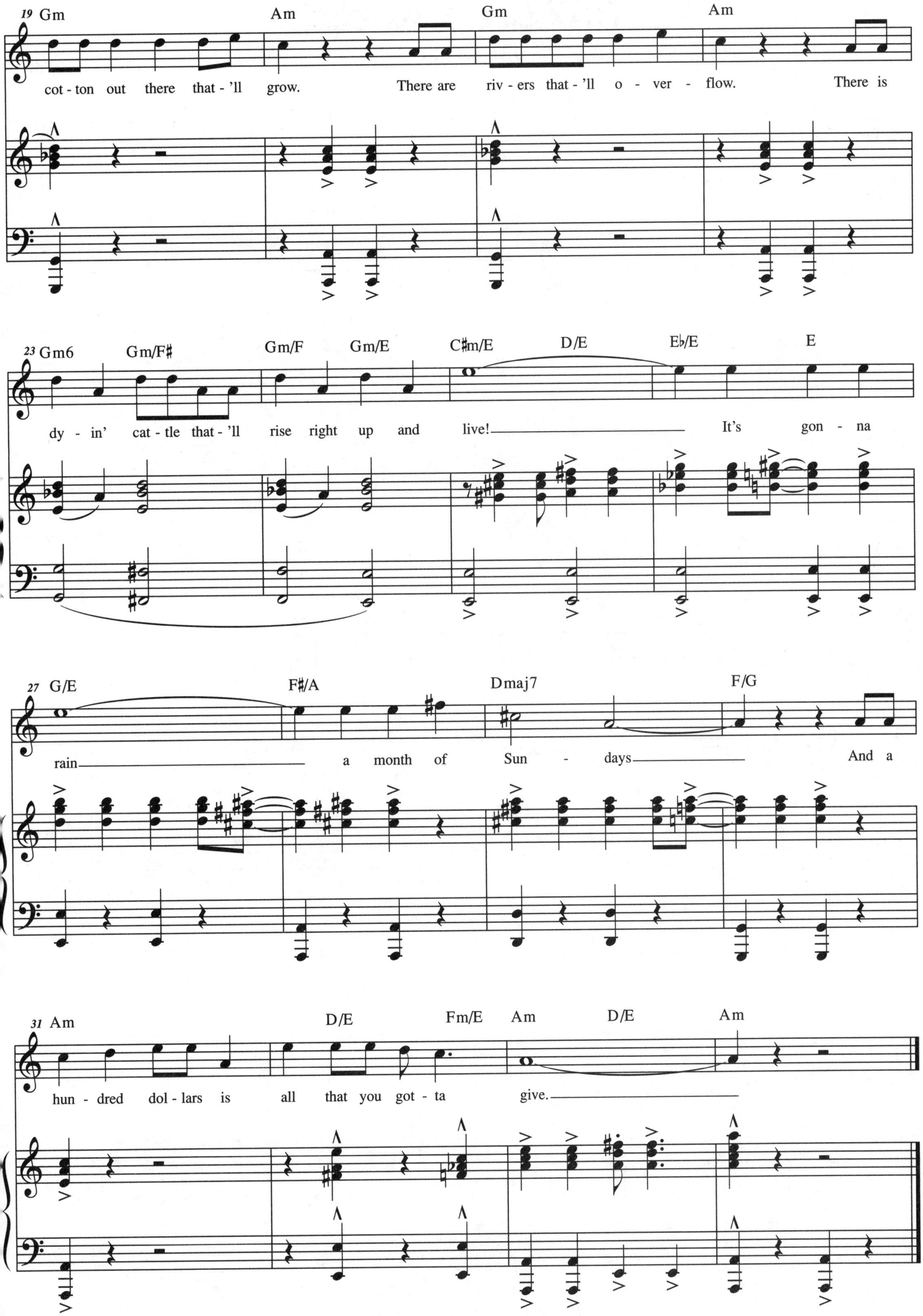
19 Gm Am Gm Am
cot - ton out there that - 'll grow. There are riv - ers that - 'll o - ver - flow. There is
23 Gm6 Gm/F♯ Gm/F Gm/E C♯m/E D/E E♭/E E
dy - in' cat - tle that - 'll rise right up and live! It's gon - na
27 G/E F♯/A Dmaj7 F/G
rain a month of Sun - days And a
31 Am D/E Fm/E Am D/E Am
hun - dred dol - lars is all that you got - ta give.

RAZZLE DAZZLE
(from "Chicago")

Words by
FRED EBB

Music by
JOHN KANDER

CD/TRACK 2/22

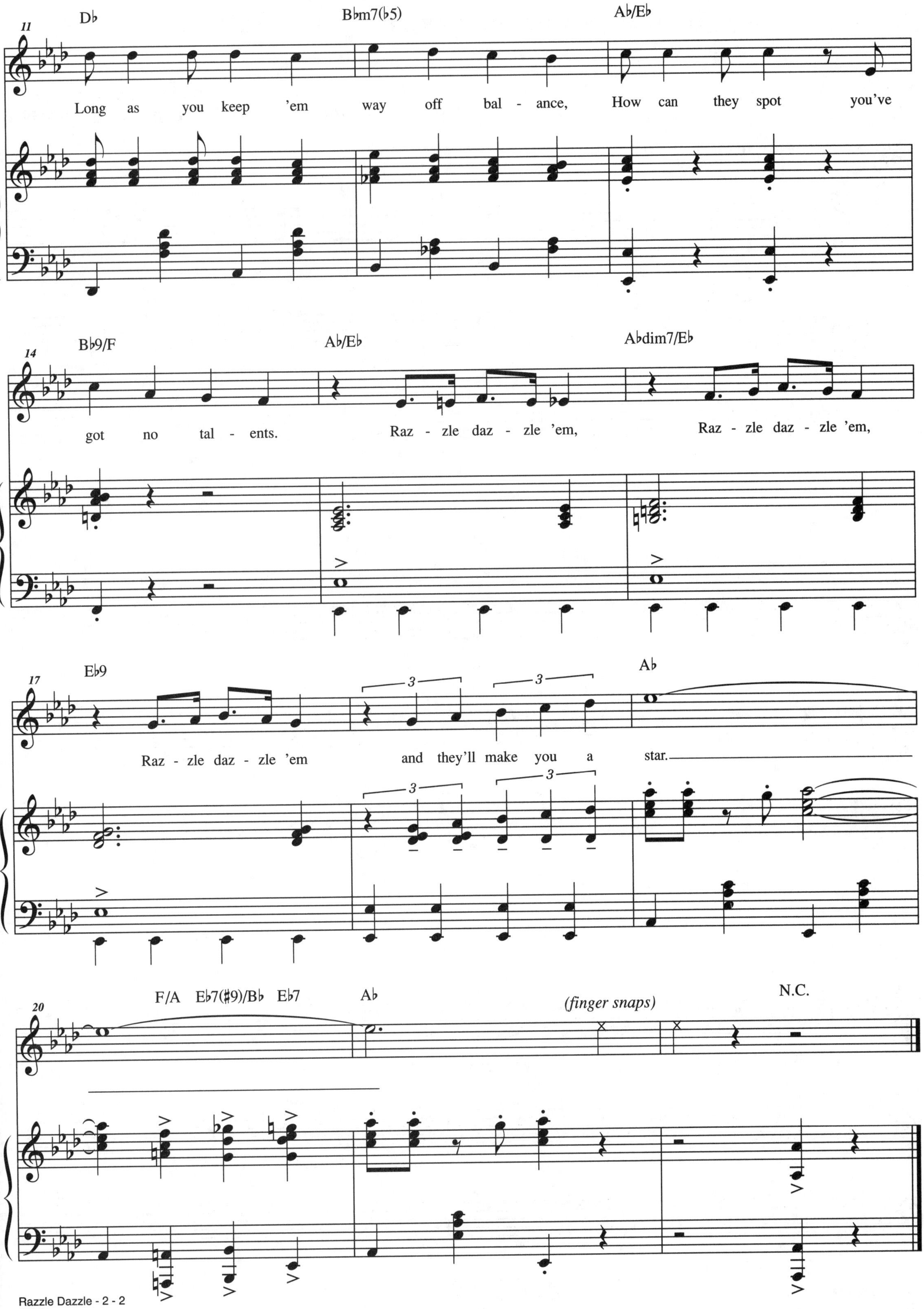
11
D♭
B♭m7(♭5)
A♭/E♭
Long as you keep 'em way off bal - ance, How can they spot you've
14
B♭9/F
A♭/E♭
A♭dim7/E♭
got no tal - ents. Raz - zle daz - zle 'em, Raz - zle daz - zle 'em,
17
E♭9
A♭
Raz - zle daz - zle 'em and they'll make you a star.
20
F/A E♭7(♯9)/B♭ E♭7
A♭
(finger snaps)
N.C.

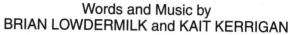

RUN AWAY WITH ME

(from "The Unauthorized Autobiography of Samantha Brown")

Words and Music by
BRIAN LOWDERMILK and KAIT KERRIGAN

* Alternate note.

SANDY
(from "Grease")

Words and Music by
LOUIS ST. LOUIS and SCOTT SIMON

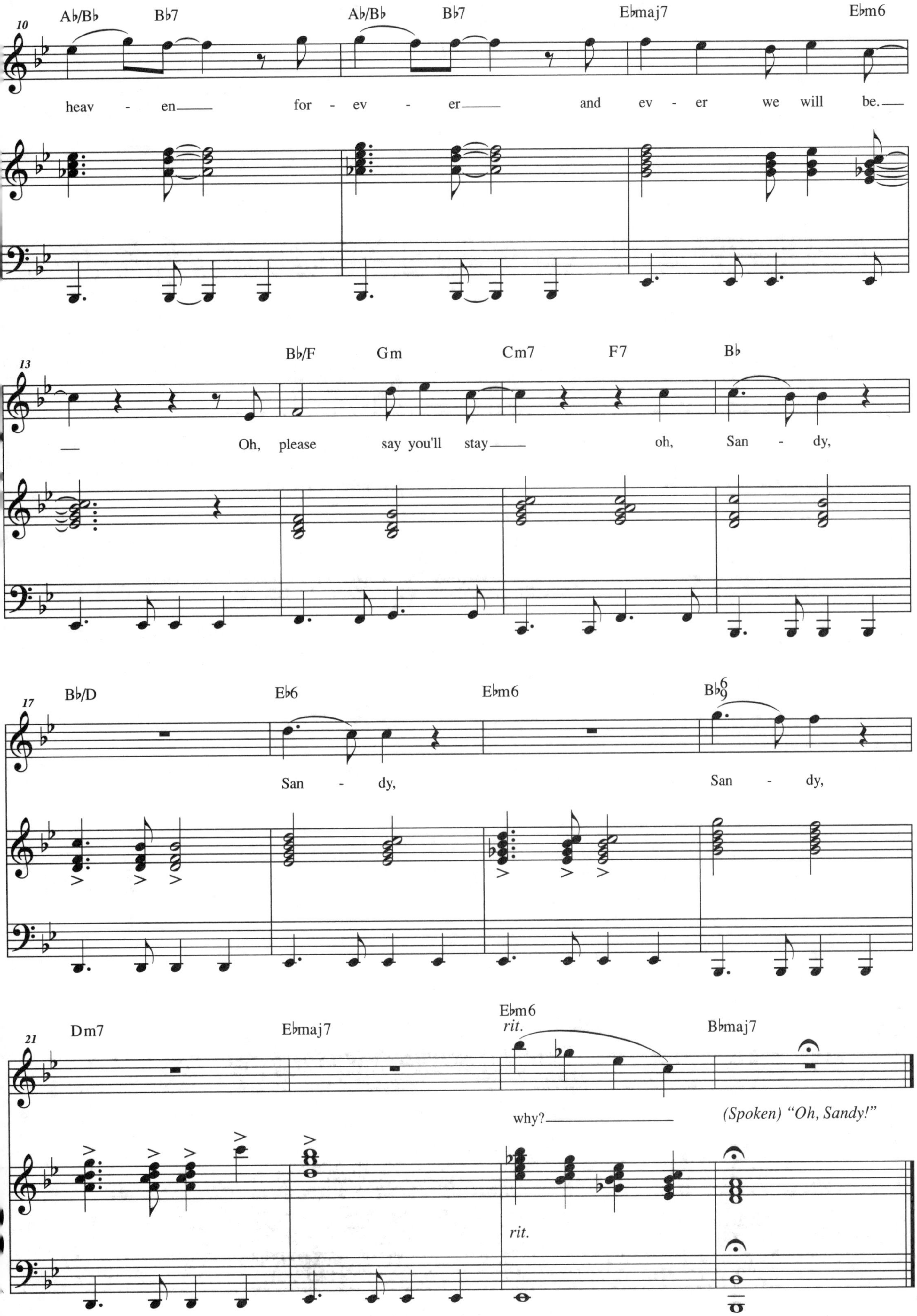
A♭/B♭
B♭7
A♭/B♭
B♭7
E♭maj7
E♭m6
heav - en
for - ev - er
and ev - er we will be.
B♭/F
Gm
Cm7
F7
B♭
Oh, please say you'll stay
oh, San - dy,
B♭/D
E♭6
E♭m6
B♭6/9
San - dy,
San - dy,
Dm7
E♭maj7
E♭m6
rit.
B♭maj7
why?
(Spoken) "Oh, Sandy!"
rit.

SINGIN' IN THE RAIN

(from "Singin' in the Rain")

Lyric by
ARTHUR FREED

Music by
NACIO HERB BROWN

19
F6
storm - y clouds chase ev - 'ry - one from the place.
23
F♯dim7
Gm6
C7
Come on with the rain; I've a smile on my face. I'll
27
Gm6
C7
Gm6
C7
walk down the lane with a hap - py re - frain. just
31
Gm6
C7
F
Gm7
B♭/C
F
sing'-in', just sing-in' in the rain.
rall.
pp

SLIDE SOME OIL TO ME

(from "The Wiz")

Words and Music by
CHARLIE SMALLS

D D7 G7
Slide some oil to me, hit my shoul - der blade.
G♯dim7 D/A B7
Come on and slide some oil down my throat and let me
E7 G/A D B7 E7 G/A
lu - bri - cate my mind, and let me lu - bri - cate my mind,
D B7 E7 G/A D
and let me lu - bri - cate my mind.
sfz

SONG OF LOVE

(from "Once Upon a Mattress")

Lyrics by
MARSHALL BARER

Music by
MARY RODGERS

CD/TRACK 2/27

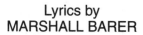

Bright 2 (𝅗𝅥 = 132)
DAUNTLESS:
mf pick up in tempo
I'm in love with a girl named Fred! My rea - sons must be clear. When she
mf
5
shows you all how strong she is you'll stand right up and cheer! I'm in love with a girl named
10
Fred! She drinks just like a lord. So come sing a mer - ry drink - ing song and

15
let the wine be poured Fill the bowl to o - ver flow - ing. Raise the gob - let
20
high. With an F and an R and an E and a D, and an F R E D Fred! I'm in
25
love with a girl, I'm in love with a girl named F -
30
- R - E - D. FRED!

THE STREETS OF DUBLIN

(from "A Man of No Importance")

Words by
LYNN AHRENS

Music by
STEPHEN FLAHERTY

E/F♯ E/G♯ E/A E/G♯ E/F♯ E Bsus/D
true feck - in' hell! Ah, you come out with me and you'll see what you're miss - in' in life
A/B E E/C♯ E/A
on the streets of Dub - lin.
Esus/D E/A Bsus E E/C♯
On the streets of Dub - lin....
E/A Esus/D A/B E
On the streets of Dub - lin.
sfz

SUDDENLY SEYMOUR
(from "Little Shop of Horrors")

Lyrics by
HOWARD ASHMAN

Music by
ALAN MENKEN

CD/TRACK 2/29

Bright rock ballad (♩ = 92)

*Alternate note.

TAKE A CHANCE ON ME

(from "Little Women")

Lyrics by
MINDI DICKSTEIN

Music by
JASON HOWLAND

16
A(add9)
Emaj9/G♯
C♯m9
A6/9
be such friends. Friends are nev - er lone - ly. All I know is books.
21
E(add9)/G♯
F♯m11
Books are sol - i - tar - y. But I see you ev - 'ry day, how you
26
E(add9)/G♯
C♯m9
Dmaj9
B7sus
F♯m7/B
live in your own way, We'll be the best of friends when you take
31
E(add9)
F♯11/E
D/G
A/G
B7sus
E
a chance on me!

TELL MY FATHER
(from "The Civil War")

Lyrics by
JACK MURPHY

Music by
FRANK WILDHORN

10
G(add9)
Dsus
D
G
G7
Tell him how I wore the Blue proud and true through the
13
Csus
C
G
fi - re. Tell my fa - ther so he'll
freely
15
Dsus
D
C/G
G
know I love him so.
(vocal cues)
freely
(with pedal)

THERE ONCE WAS A MAN

(from "Pajama Game")

CD/TRACK 2/32

Words and Music by
RICHARD ADLER and JERRY ROSS

Up-tempo (𝅗𝅥 = 152–160)

*Alternate note.

THEY CAN'T TAKE THAT AWAY FROM ME

(from "Crazy for You")

Music and Lyrics by GEORGE GERSHWIN
and IRA GERSHWIN

CD/TRACK 2/33

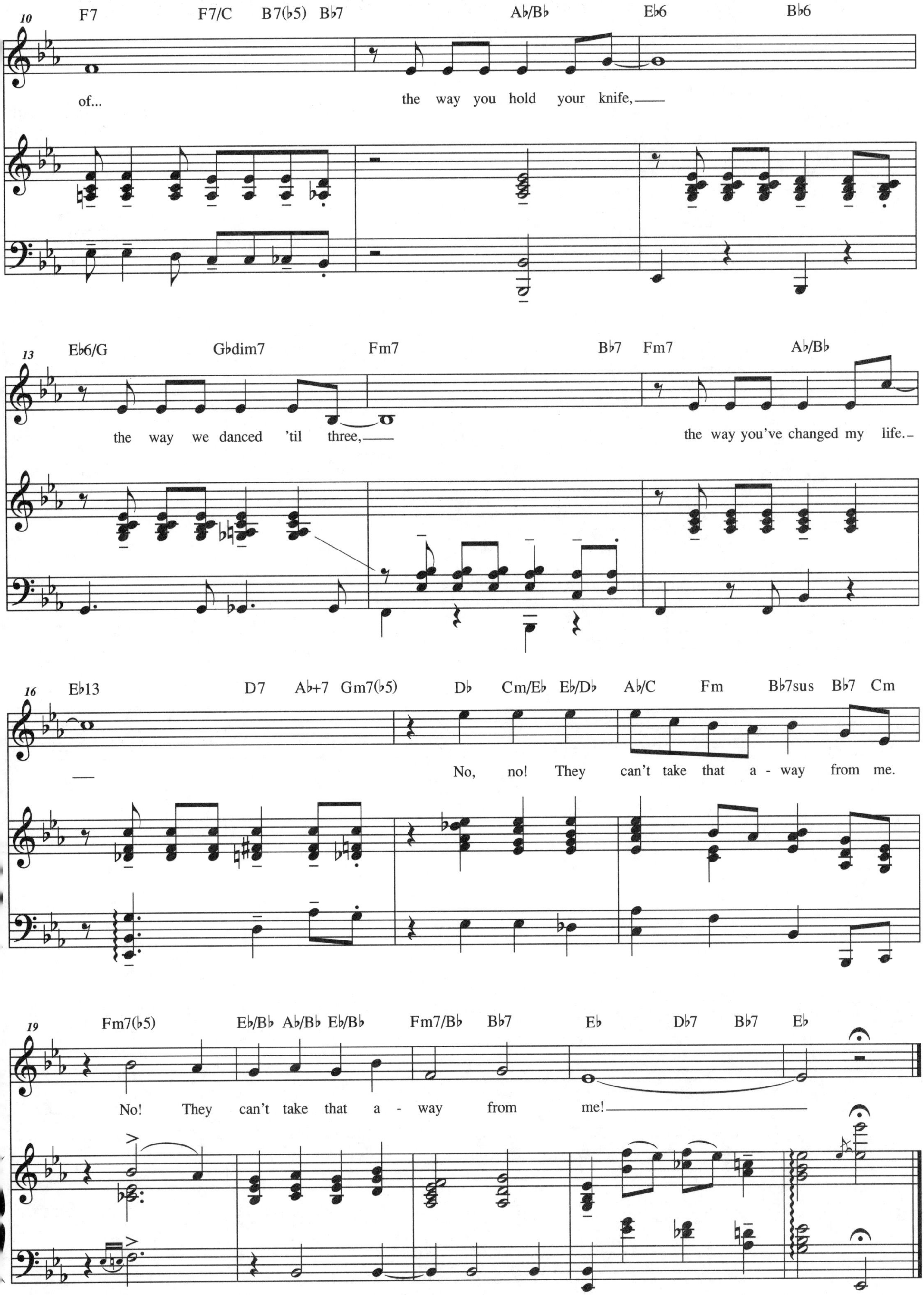
10
F7 F7/C B7(♭5) B♭7 A♭/B♭ E♭6 B♭6
of... the way you hold your knife,
13
E♭6/G G♭dim7 Fm7 B♭7 Fm7 A♭/B♭
the way we danced 'til three, the way you've changed my life.
16
E♭13 D7 A♭+7 Gm7(♭5) D♭ Cm/E♭ E♭/D♭ A♭/C Fm B♭7sus B♭7 Cm
No, no! They can't take that a - way from me.
19
Fm7(♭5) E♭/B♭ A♭/B♭ E♭/B♭ Fm7/B♭ B♭7 E♭ D♭7 B♭7 E♭
No! They can't take that a - way from me!

THEY WERE YOU

(from "The Fantasticks")

Lyrics by
HARVEY SCHMIDT

Music by
TOM JONES

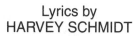

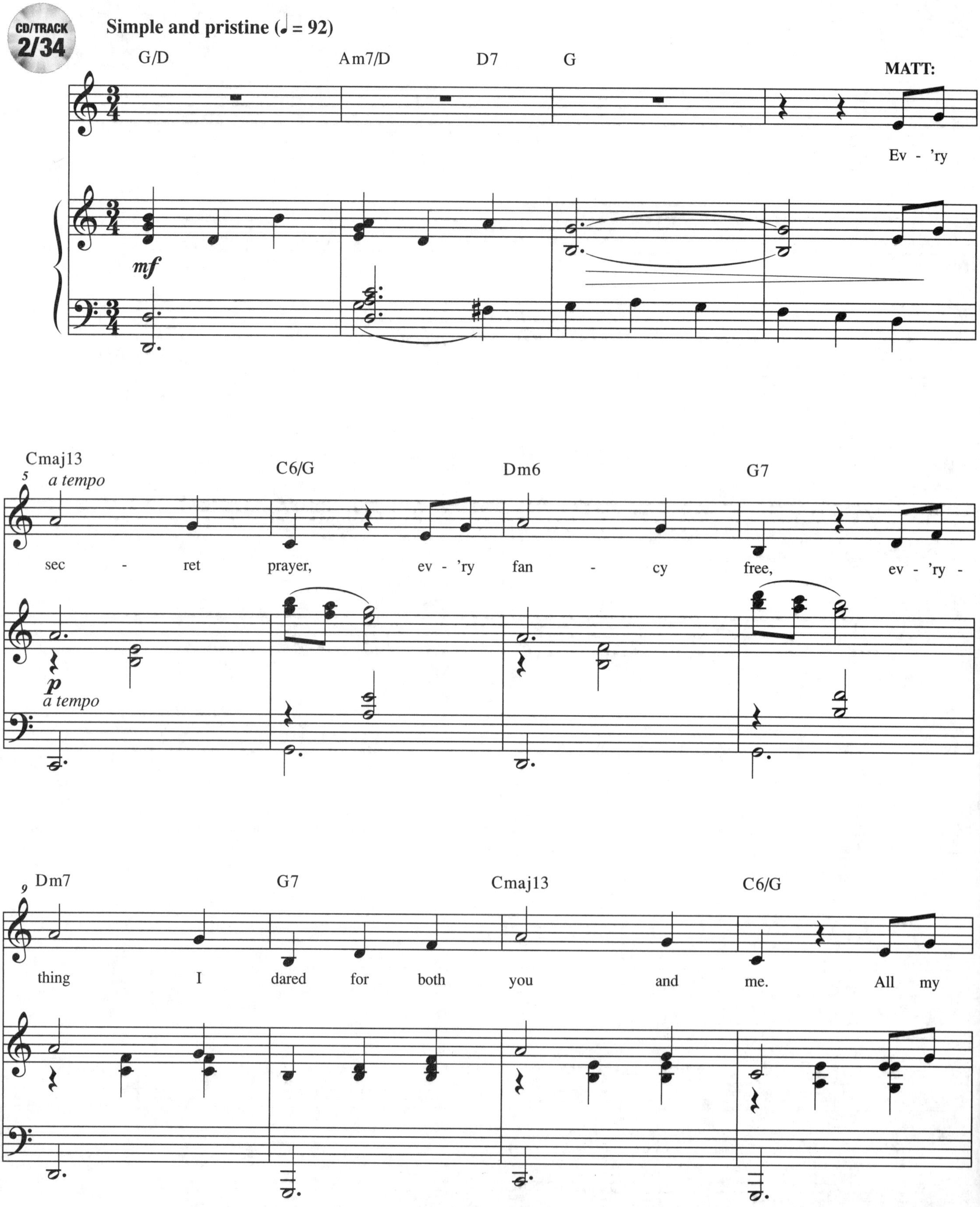

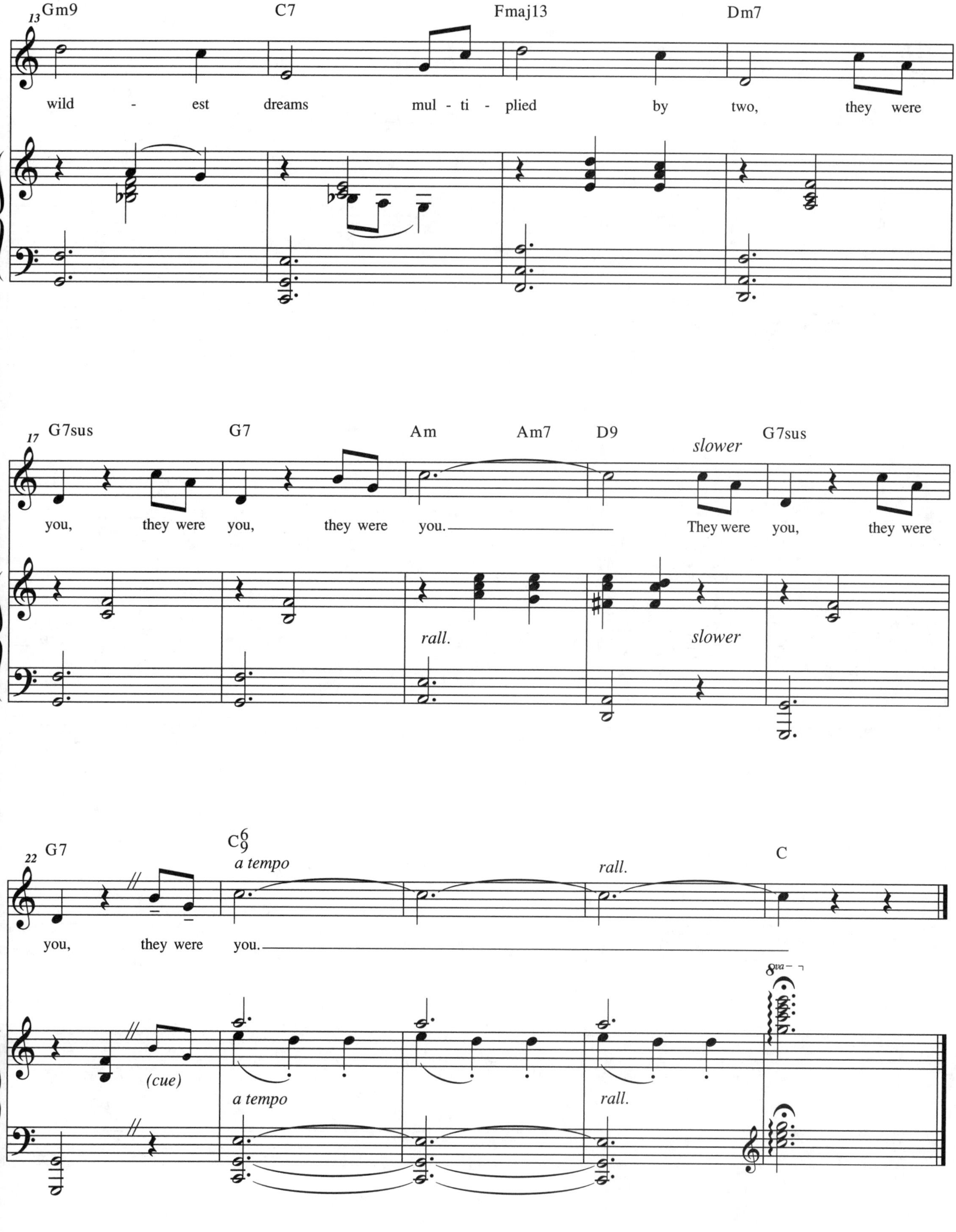
13
Gm9
C7
Fmaj13
Dm7
wild - est dreams mul - ti - plied by two, they were
17
G7sus
G7
Am
Am7
D9
slower
G7sus
you, they were you, they were you. They were you, they were
rall.
slower
22
G7
C6/9
a tempo
rall.
C
you, they were you.
8va
(cue)
a tempo
rall.

THOSE WERE THE GOOD OLD DAYS

(from "Damn Yankees")

Words and Music by
RICHARD ADLER and JERRY ROSS

Moderate, light rocking (♩ = 92)

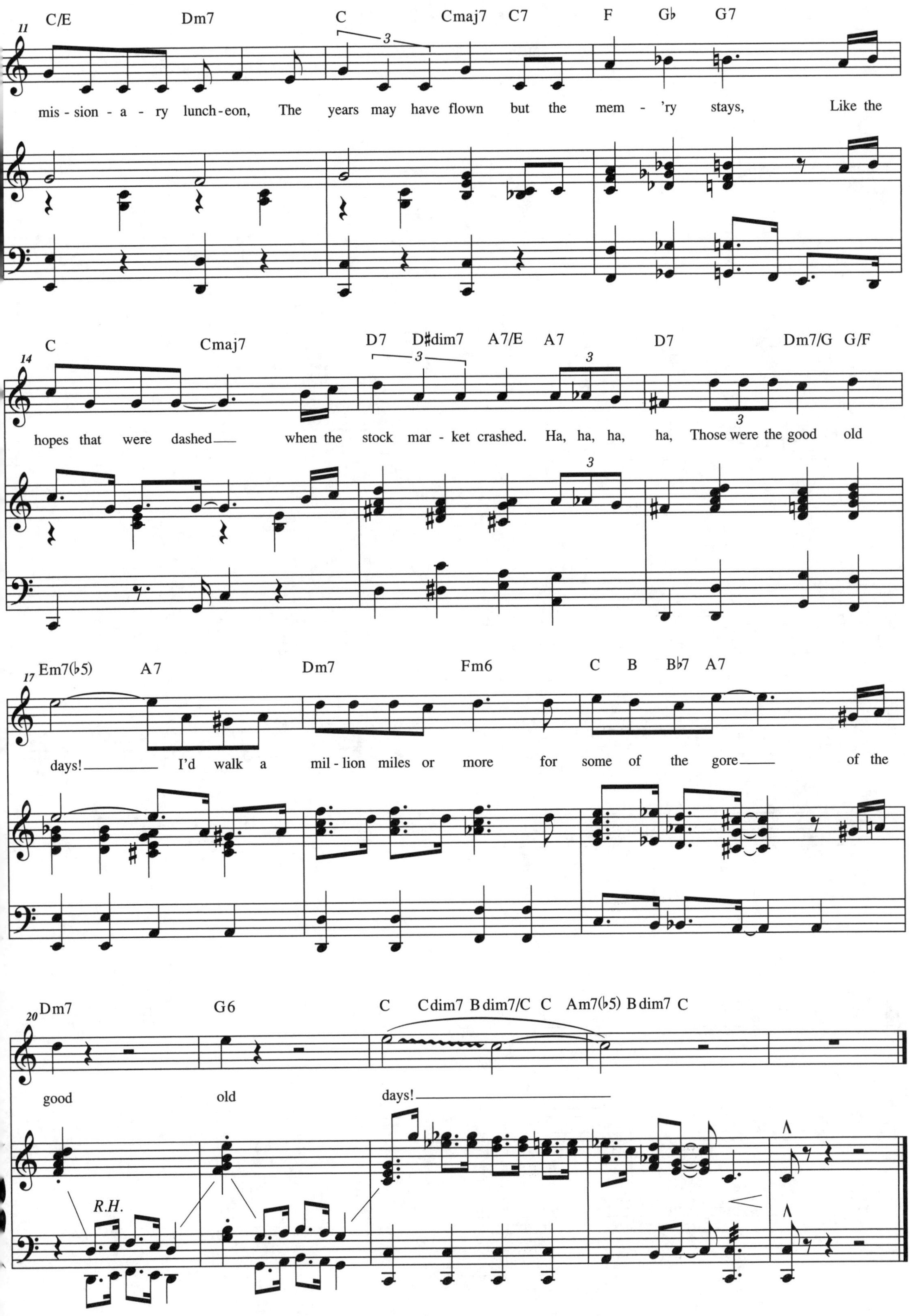
11
C/E Dm7 C Cmaj7 C7 F G♭ G7
mis - sion - a - ry lunch - eon, The years may have flown but the mem - 'ry stays, Like the
14
C Cmaj7 D7 D♯dim7 A7/E A7 D7 Dm7/G G/F
hopes that were dashed when the stock mar - ket crashed. Ha, ha, ha, ha, Those were the good old
17
Em7(♭5) A7 Dm7 Fm6 C B B♭7 A7
days! I'd walk a mil - lion miles or more for some of the gore of the
20
Dm7 G6 C Cdim7 Bdim7/C C Am7(♭5) Bdim7 C
good old days!
R.H.

TOO DARN HOT
(from "Kiss Me Kate")

Words and Music by
COLE PORTER

CD/TRACK 2/36
Allegro (𝅗𝅥 = 100)
Em Bm7 Em B7 E D♯7 E
PAUL:
mf
Ac - cord - ing to the Kin - sey re - port, ev - 'ry
5
D♯7 E
av - er - age man you know much pre - fers to play his fa - vour - ite sport when the
9
B7 E E7 A E A D♯7/A♯
tem - per - a - ture is low. But when the ther - mom - e - ter goes 'way up and the

13
E/B A E/G♯ C♯7 F♯7 B7 E A C/B♭ B7
weath-er is sizz - lin' hot, Mis - ter Gob, for his squab, a ma -
17
E A C/B♭ B7 E A C/B♭ B7
rine for his queen, a G. I. for his cut - ie - pie is
21
E N.C. Em Bm7 Em
not, 'cause it's too, too, too darn hot, it's
25
Em Bm7 Em Am B+ Em
too darn hot, it's too darn hot!
8va

WAIT TILL WE'RE SIXTY-FIVE

(from "On a Clear Day You Can See Forever")

Words by
ALAN JAY LERNER

Music by
BURTON LANE

21
C C♯dim7 G9/D
Six years or sev-en, then to heav-en; Me first, the rec - ords show. You get the pen-sion,
26
C♯dim7 G9/D C♯dim7 Dm7 G7 Am7 B♭(add9) C7
not to men-tion Blue Cross un-til you go. If you ev - er thought you had
31
Fmaj7 Fm C/E Cmaj7 C6 D9 D+9
fun at twen - ty one, wait till we're six -
37
Dm7/G G7(♭9) C Cm7 B♭m7/G G13 C
ty - five.

WHAT AM I DOIN'?

(from "Closer Than Ever")

Words by
RICHARD MALTBY, JR.

Music by
DAVID SHIRE

CD/TRACK 2/38
Moderate (♩ = 80)
A♭m7 B♭m7 A♭m7 B♭m7
Then she
mp
3 A♭m7 B♭m7 A♭m7 B♭m7
sud - den - ly said I can't see her. And the
5 A♭m7 B♭m7 A♭m7 B♭m7
thought of it drove me in - sane. So I
7 Bm7 C♯m7 Bm7 C♯m7
find up a tree I am creep - ing, To the roof o - ver where she is sleep - ing. And I

*Alternate note.

WHAT DO I NEED WITH LOVE

(from "Thoroughly Modern Millie")

Lyrics by
DICK SCANLAN

Music by
JEANINE TESORI

13
G6 C9 G6 G♯dim7
In a row I have my ducks.
Loads of gals to give me loads of yuks.
17
D7 B♭7 B+7 C7 C♯+7
Leave the coo - ing to the oth - er clucks.
I don't mean may - be.
21
A9 D7 Bm7(♭5) E
Got it good.
What do I need with love?
I
25
A9 D7 G
got it good.
What do I need with love?

WHAT WOULD I DO IF I COULD FEEL?

(from "The Wiz")

Words and Music by
CHARLIE SMALLS

CD/TRACK 2/40

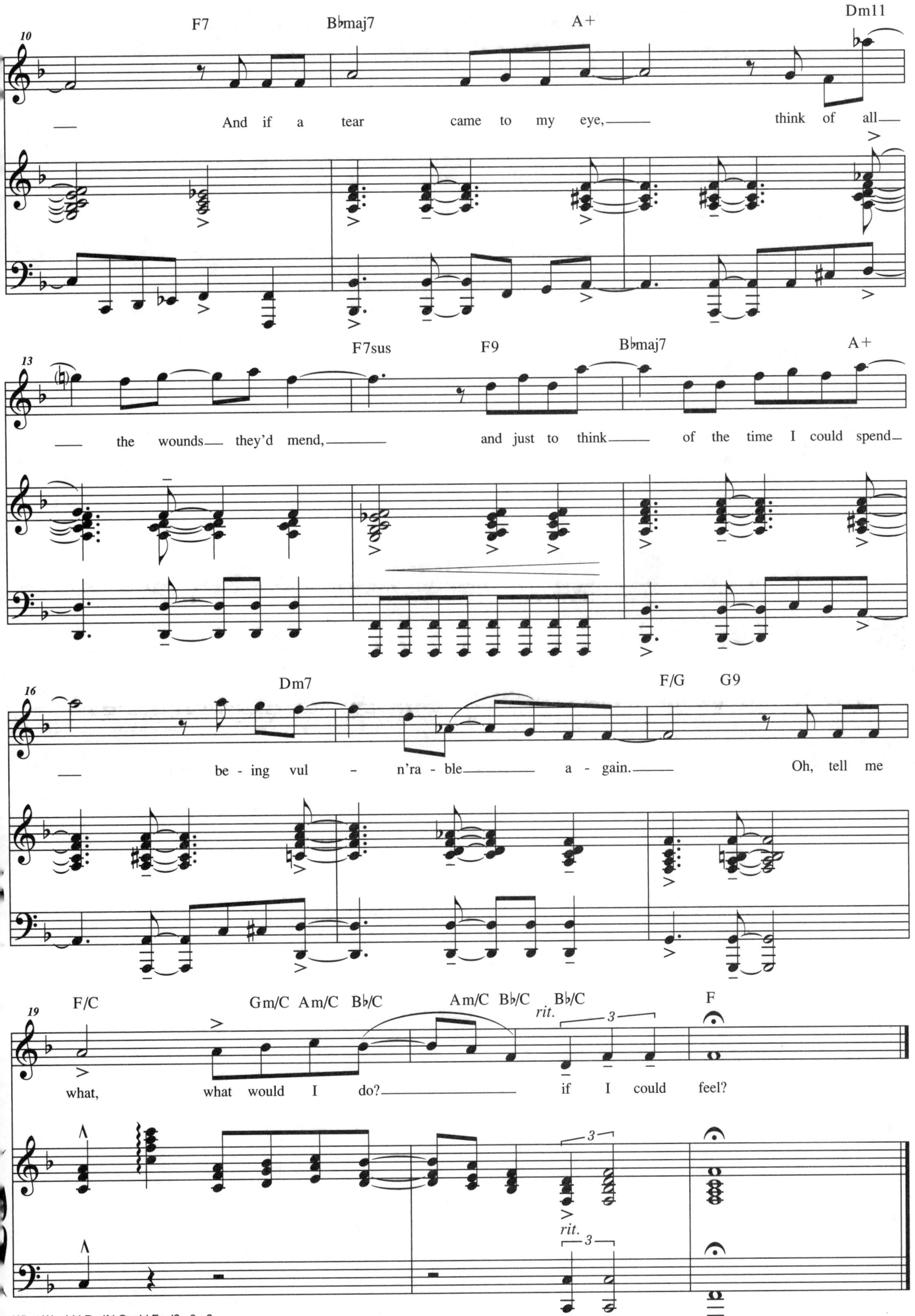
10
F7
B♭maj7
A+
Dm11
And if a tear came to my eye, think of all
13
F7sus
F9
B♭maj7
A+
the wounds they'd mend, and just to think of the time I could spend
16
Dm7
F/G
G9
being vul - n'ra - ble a - gain. Oh, tell me
19
F/C
Gm/C Am/C B♭/C
Am/C B♭/C
B♭/C
F
rit.
3
what, what would I do? if I could feel?
rit.
3

THE WHEELS OF A DREAM

(from "Ragtime")

Lyrics by
LYNN AHRENS

Music by
STEPHEN FLAHERTY

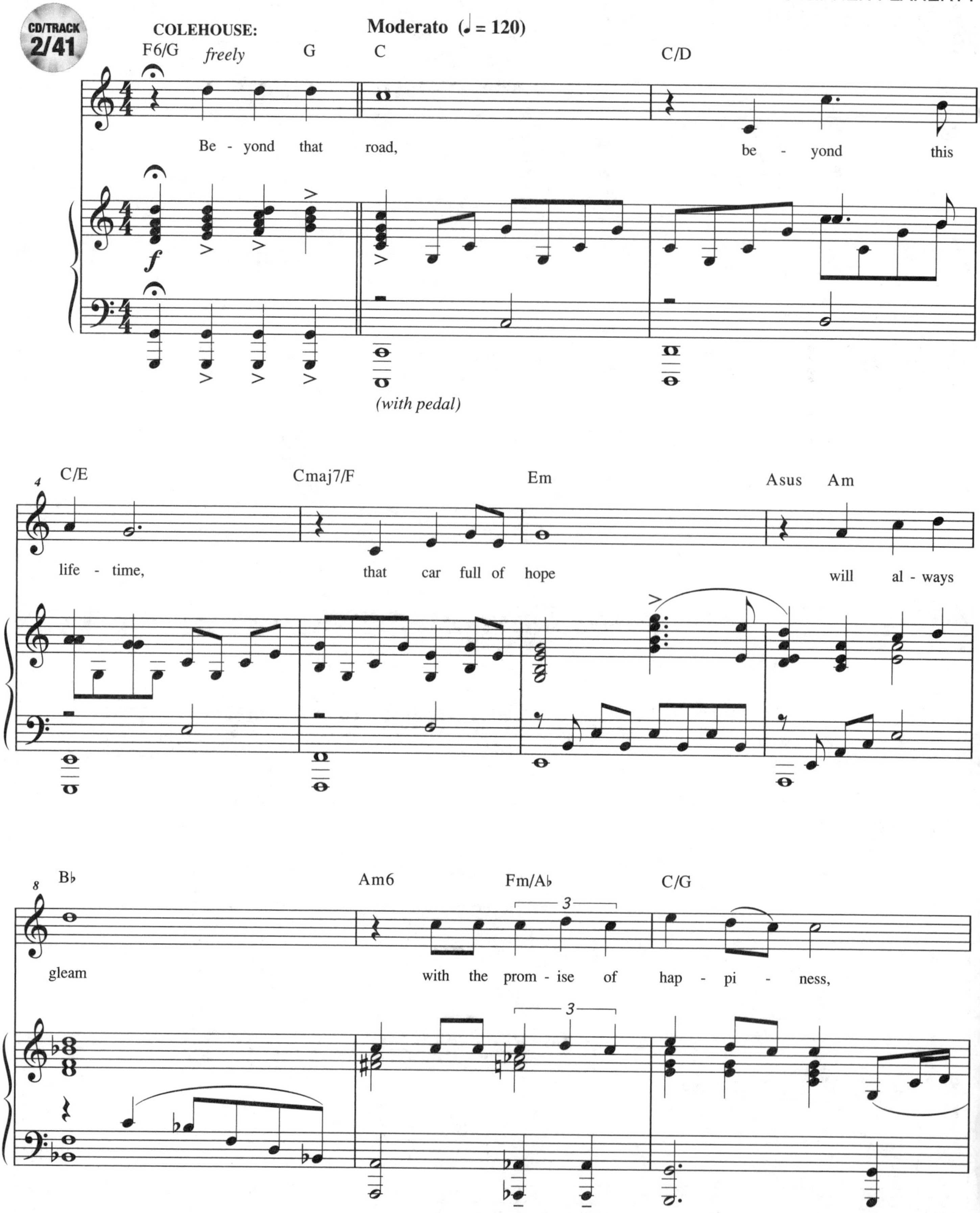

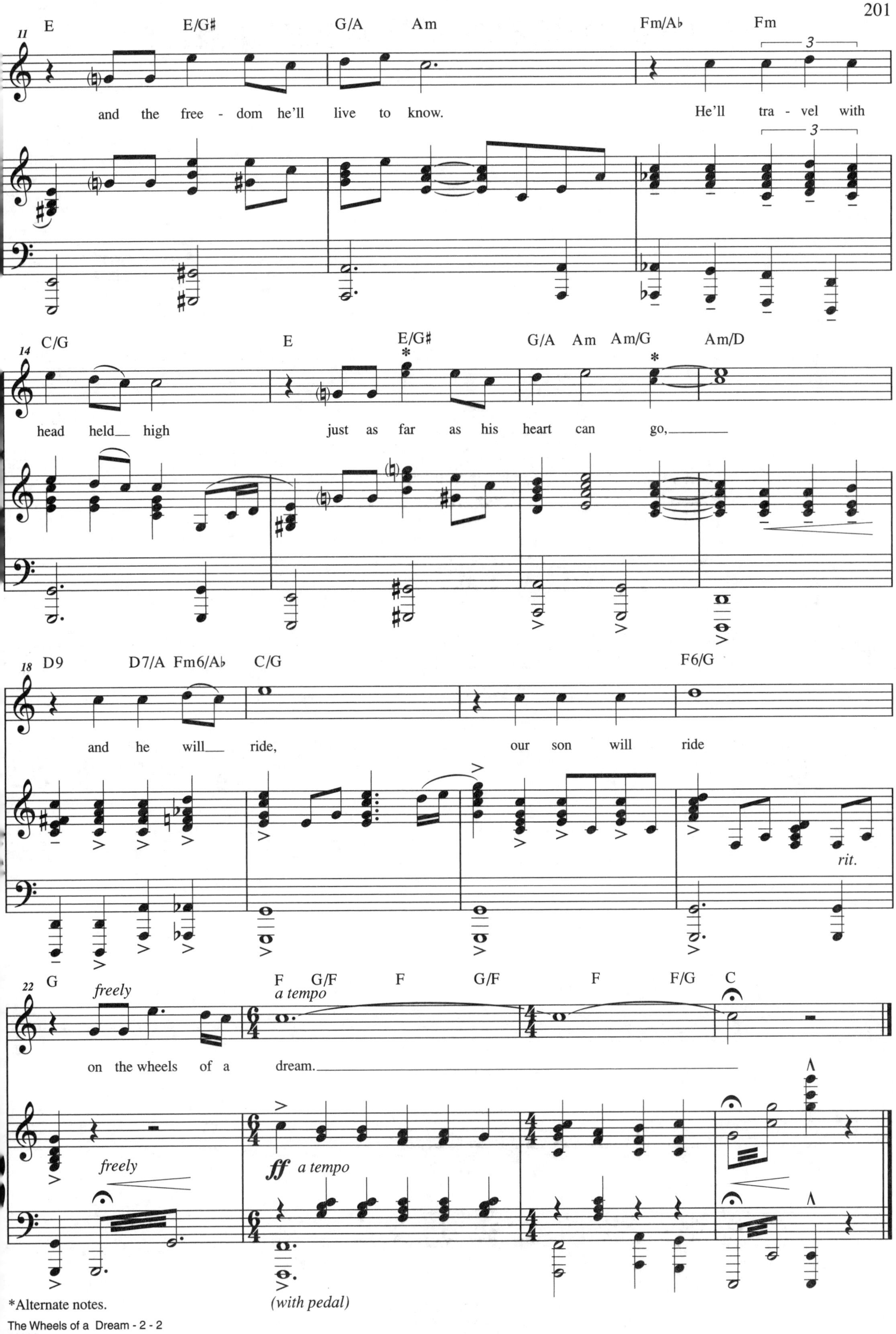

*Alternate notes.

WHEN I GET MY NAME IN LIGHTS

(from "The Boy from Oz")

Words and Music by
PETER ALLEN

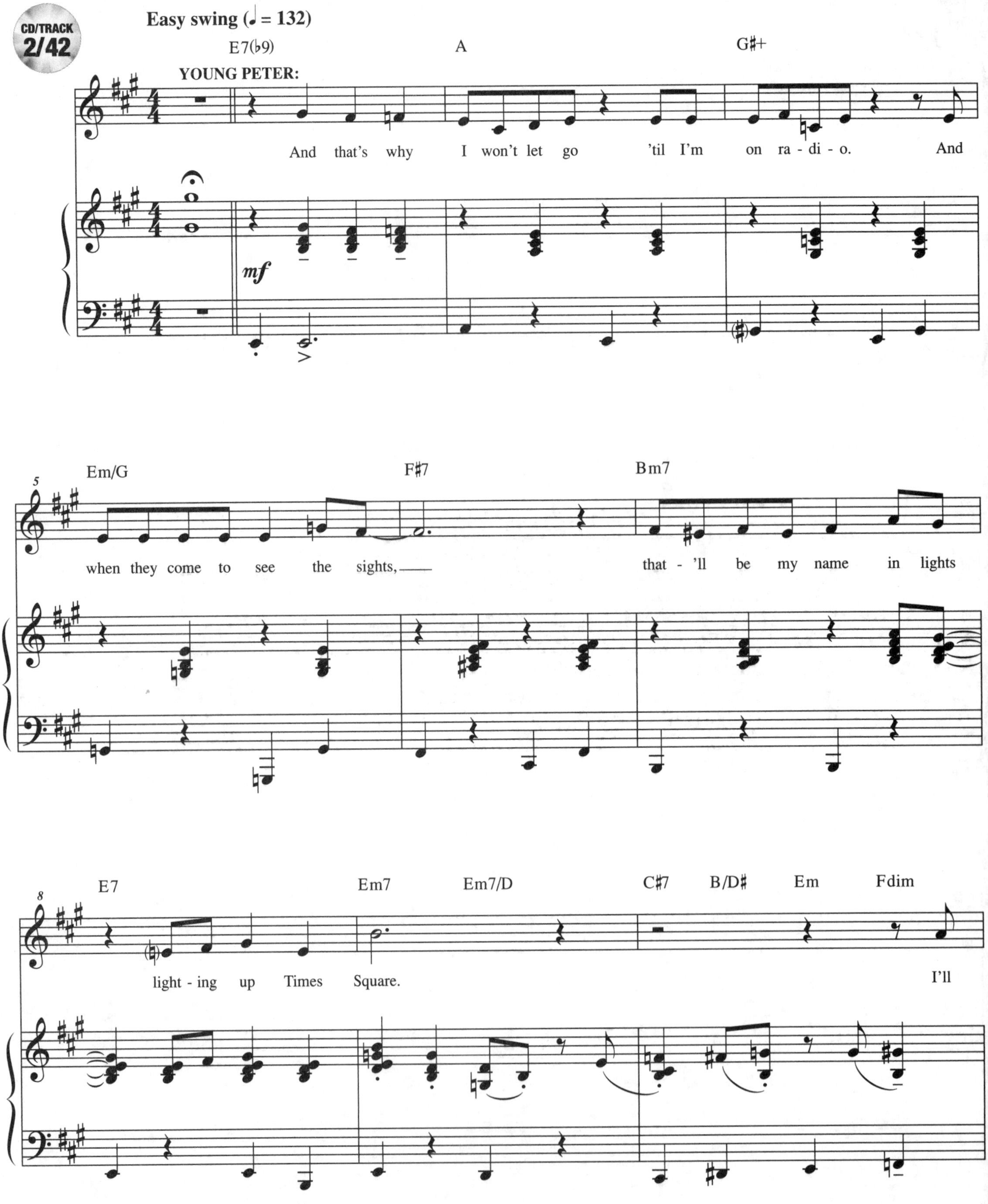

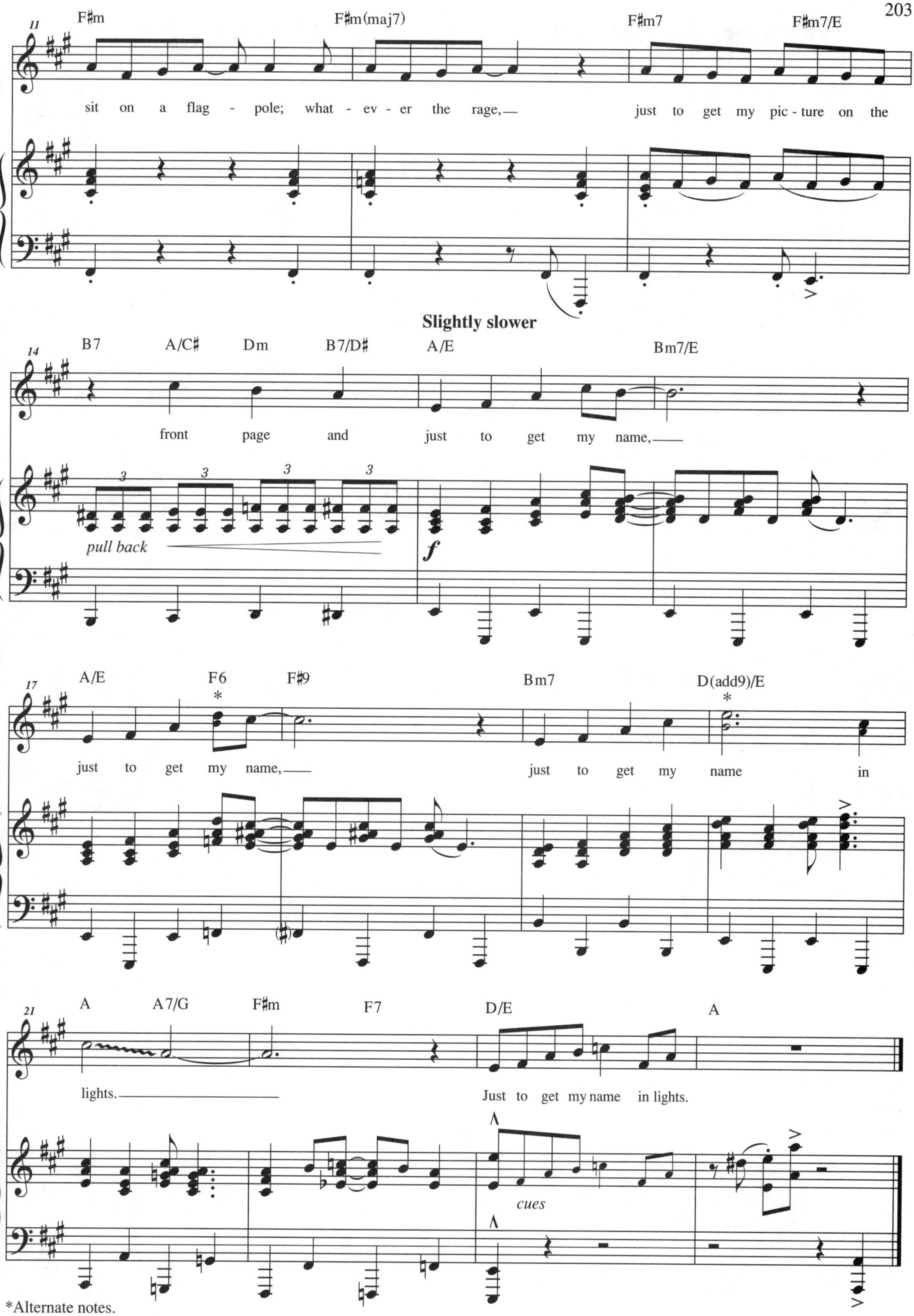

*Alternate notes.

WHEN I'M NOT NEAR THE GIRL I LOVE

(from "Finian's Rainbow")

Words by
E.Y. HARBURG

Music by
BURTON LANE

Freely
21
Ebm7
Bbm/Ab
Ebm7
a tempo
Sha - ron I'm car - in', but Su - zan I'm choo - sin'. I'm faith - ful to
a tempo
26
Ab7
F7sus
Bb7
Ebm7
Gbm6
whos - 'n is here. When I'm not near the
31
Db/F
Edim7
Db/Ab
Ebm7/Ab
girl I love, I love the girl
36
Gb/Ab
Db
Gb/Ab
Db
I'm near!
sfz
sfz

WHERE DO I GO?

(from "Hair")

Lyrics by
JAMES RADO
and GEROME RAGNI

Music by
GALT MacDERMOT

CD/TRACK 2/44

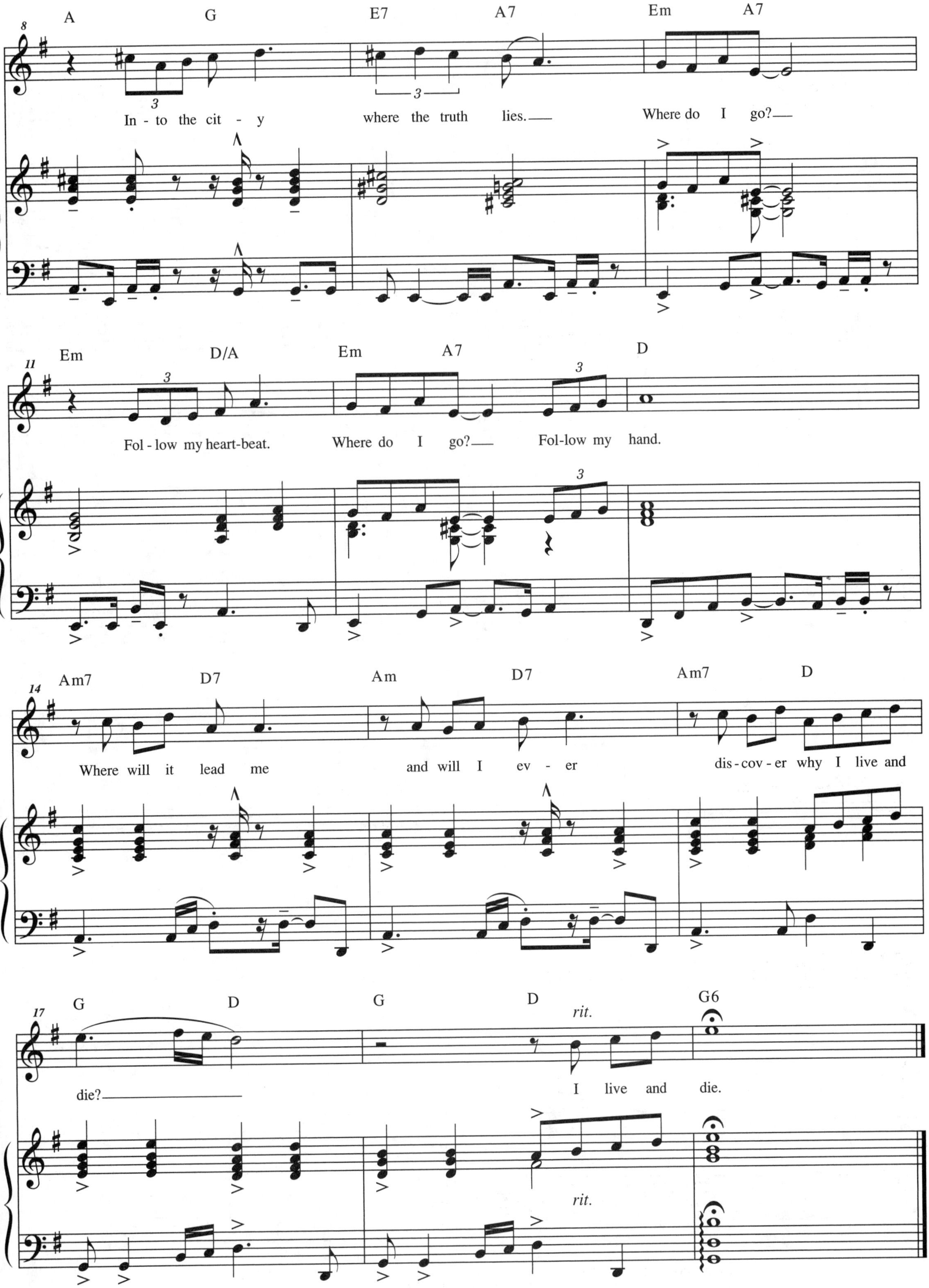
A G E7 A7 Em A7
In - to the cit - y where the truth lies. Where do I go?
Em D/A Em A7 D
Fol - low my heart-beat. Where do I go? Fol-low my hand.
Am7 D7 Am D7 Am7 D
Where will it lead me and will I ev - er dis - cov - er why I live and
G D G D rit. G6
die? I live and die.
rit.

WHO I'D BE

(from "Shrek: The Musical")

Words by
DAVID LINDSAY-ABAIRE

Music by
JEANINE TESORI

CD/TRACK 2/45

* Lower note (E♭) optional.

WINTER'S ON THE WING

(from "The Secret Garden")

Lyrics by
MARSHA NORMAN

Music by
LUCY SIMON

CD/TRACK
2/46

Light, sturdy folk-rock (♩ = 80)

Dm7
C♯7
F♯7sus
DICKSON:
And now the
Bm7
E(add9)
G
G/A
mist is lift-in' high leav-in' bright blue air rol-lin' clear 'cross the moor comes the May I say. The
8va
Bm7
E(add9)
G
A
Bsus
B7
storm-'ll soon be by leav-in' clear blue sky. Soon the sun will shine comes the day say I. And
8va
E
D/E
C♯m/E
D/E
A
D/A
A
D/A
A
you'll be here to see it. Stand and

9 E D/E C♯m/E D/E C♯7sus
breathe it all the day.
11 F♯ F♯/A♯ B(add9) E E/G♯ A(add9)
Stoop and feel it. Stop and hear it.
13 F♯7sus
Spring, I
8va
15 B7 G(add9) N.C. B
say!

WITH YOU
(from "Pippin")

Music and Lyrics by
STEPHEN SCHWARTZ

CD/TRACK 2/47

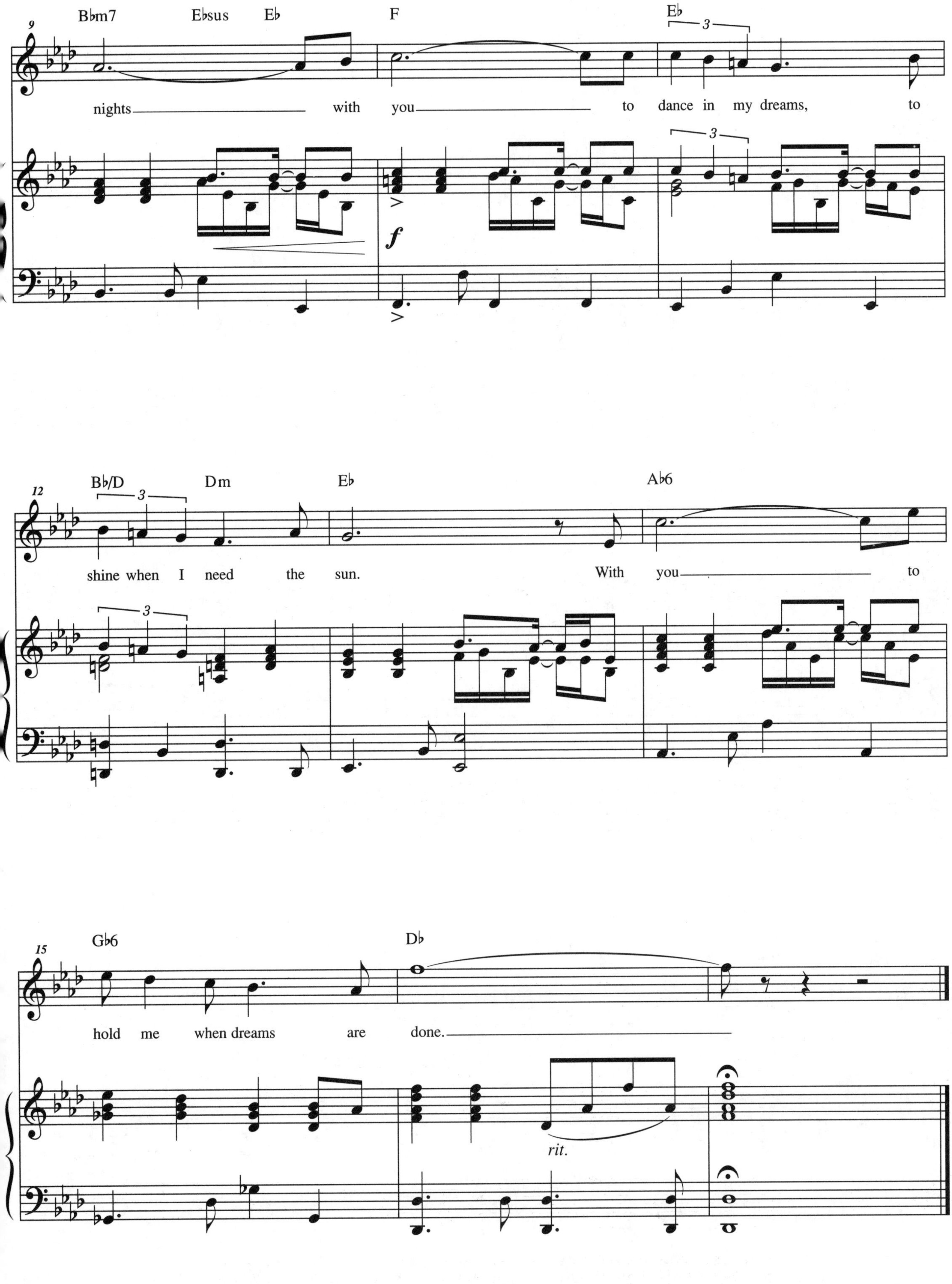
9
Bbm7 Ebsus Eb F Eb
nights with you to dance in my dreams, to
f
12
Bb/D Dm Eb Ab6
shine when I need the sun. With you to
15
Gb6 Db
hold me when dreams are done.
rit.

YOU ARE MY HOME

(from "The Scarlet Pimpernel")

Words by
NAN KNIGHTON

Music by
FRANK WILDHORN

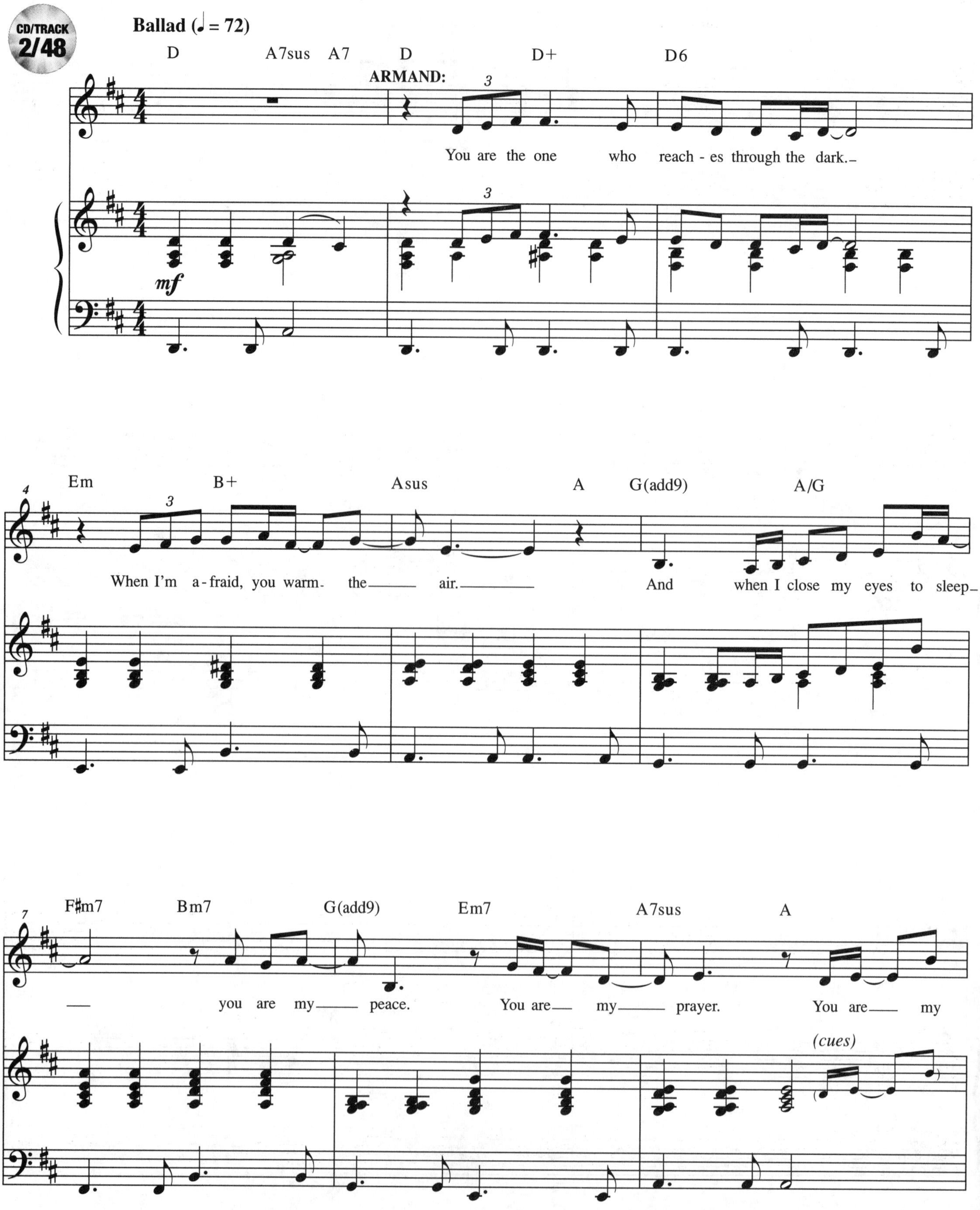

*Alternate note.

YOU MUSTN'T KICK IT AROUND

(from "Pal Joey")

Words by
LORENZ HART

Music by
RICHARD RODGERS

CD/TRACK 2/49

13
E♭7 A♭6 F7 B♭maj7
when we have a brawl, if I turn the oth - er cheek,
17
B♭7 E♭7 A♭ A♭m7
you must-n't kick it at all. When I try to ring the bell,
21
E♭7/B♭ A♭ E♭m7 A♭7 D♭ D♭m7
you nev - er care for the sound. The next guy may not do as well;
25
E♭13 E13 E♭7 A♭
you must - n't kick it a - round.

YOU'RE GETTING TO BE A HABIT WITH ME

(from "42nd Street")

Words by
AL DUBIN

Music by
HARRY WARREN

CD/TRACK 2/50

Moderate swing (♩ = 112)

Em/G G7 C7 F7 B♭ C7
need you for my own. Oh, I can't break a - way. I must
B♭ C7 F E7/B B♭7 A7 D7
have you ev - 'ry day; as reg - u - lar - ly as cof - fee or tea. You've
Gm E7 A7 D7 F♯dim7 Gm G7 C7
got me in your clutch - es, and I can't get free; you're get - ting to be a hab - it with
F A7/E Am7 D7 F♯dim Gm C7 F6
me, (can't break it!) You're get - ting to be a hab - it with me.
rall.
8va

Alfred